50

MORE STORIES

and

SONGS

50
MORE STORIES
and
SONGS

JAMES D. WOOD

iUniverse®

50 MORE STORIES AND SONGS

The author expresses thanks for the use of the poem: "What is a Veteran?" by Anthony Barton Hinkle. It is published with permission from the Richmond Times-Dispatch, where this first appeared.

iUniverse books may be ordered through booksellers or by contacting:

iUniverse
1663 Liberty Drive
Bloomington, IN 47403
www.iuniverse.com
1-800-Authors (1-800-288-4677)

ISBN: 978-1-5320-6683-2 (sc)
ISBN: 978-1-5320-6682-5 (e)

Library of Congress Control Number: 2019900935

Print information available on the last page.

iUniverse rev. date: 02/05/2019

Dedication

for my children
Danita, Jim, and Kathryn

Contents

Introduction

AFTER PUBLISHING *THIS IS MY STORY, This Is My Song: A Minister's Memoir* in the latter part of 2012, it sold more than two hundred and fifty copies. Another fifty copies were given to family and friends. Though my intention in writing some of my life's stories was mainly for our children and grandchildren, I since have been asked by several persons, "When are you going to write another book?" I'm not sure I want to go through that unbearable ordeal again. It was George Orwell who said, "Writing a book is a horrible, exhausting struggle, like a long bout with some painful illness. One would never undertake such a thing if one were not driven on by some demon whom one can neither resist nor understand."

I'm not sure about the demon part; however, I have recalled some personal events that I had forgotten. I remembered this and I recollected that, and I thought, *Well, why didn't you include that experience? How could you overlook that time in your life?* Therefore, I began writing again. Moreover, I wrote some more.

In my memoir, I structured its contents into short chapters or vignettes, naming some sections after musical terms or parts of a worship service. In *50 More Stories and Songs,* I have *refrained* (get it?) from doing the same but have included some sermons as well as closing each narrative with the words of a hymn. This latter is sometimes contained within a story, but usually, it will appear at the end of each account. For the most part, each hymn corresponds with the intent or theme of the writing. This writing is primarily a work of non-fiction. The only exception lies within the narrative on pages 35-36. All the words of these hymns are within the public domain, and I have included the author's name and year of composition. You, the reader, may see the relationship clearly. However, in some cases, the correlation lies exclusively within my strange mind. As one clever feature writer for our local newspaper used to say, "Try not to worry about it."

Even with these additional stories, the memoir is still incomplete because my story and my song continue to develop every day that I am privileged to enjoy the gift of life—God's gift of life. I'm a person filled to the brim with gratitude to God for the many blessings God has bestowed upon me. This joyful attitude of gratitude has imparted other beneficial characteristics to me. I view myself as one who is hopeful, gracious, generous, self-aware, calming, and a good historian regarding my own life. I share the following in the hope that you will see some of these qualities in yourself. You, too, are a child of God. I encourage you to go out and boldly claim that incredible legacy and inheritance!

1

Baptism Renewal at Oscar's

OSCAR'S RESTAURANT AND DRIVE-IN has a special place in my life. Located on National Avenue, the central north and south street in National City, California, Oscar's was a local hangout (yes, we used that word in ancient times) for the high school crowd. It served hamburgers, french fries, and malts and an assortment of greasy, artery strangling foods that would create health problems later on in our lives. If anyone knew of the adverse results of eating these "wonderfully delicious delights" at that time, the studies weren't made available to the public.

Another hangout for the high school kids in our community was a similar drive-in called Keith's. Its location was in the northern section of National City across the street from the Bay Theater. At one point in time, both restaurants were managed by members of our local Methodist Church—Keith's by Howard McMillen and Oscar's by Lawson Martin. My wife Martha and I preferred eating at Oscar's, and it was here in early 1957 where a small church group of high school and college-age youth were gathered. Martha was among them, and I asked her if she needed a ride home. Fortunately, she was so taken aback by my unexpected question that she consented. Thus, our courtship began, and the rest is history.

Fast-forward some six years. The year is 1963. My military obligation and time on active duty with the U.S. Navy is complete. We have been married for almost four years, our first child is three-years-old, and Martha is pregnant with our second child. Both of us are singing in the church choir, along with Martha's mother, and she has taken to inviting us for Sunday dinner at Oscar's following each Sunday's worship service.

One particular Sunday, Martha's mother graciously offers to treat us once again to dinner at Oscar's. Lawson Martin greets us as we enter the restaurant, along with our toddler daughter Danita, and escorts us to a table. We scrutinize the menus, but I already know what I am going to order. The shrimp dinner at Oscar's is superb. Jumbo prawns, spicy cocktail sauce, french fries, and a large wedge of lettuce with Thousand Island dressing makes my mouth water. That's my order. Iced tea is my preference for a beverage, but water with ice is always served. What happens next is the reason for my inclusion in this story.

Our waitress (nowadays the term is "food server") greets each of us and proceeds to place a glass of ice water in front of us. Since I'm the only male figure at our table, she serves me last and promptly spills my full glass of water all over my lap. Everyone is speechless, though an audible gasp comes from each of us, including our waitress. She is horrified and apologizes. "It's only water," I say and try to ease her concerns. "It will dry out."

She is evidently embarrassed and leaves returning with a clean rag to mop up the table. Another employee comes over to wipe the floor while we move our feet to facilitate his job. I quietly chuckle to those at our table and hope my pants dry before we leave the restaurant.

Our waitress returns with another glass of ice water, again apologizing for the mishap. I see that she is a little unnerved as she starts to place the glass in front of me once more. Then it happens! She accidentally (I'm giving her the benefit of the doubt) tips the water glass again!

I jump and try to avoid a cascade of water and ice cubes moving toward me, but my reaction is too slow. I'm drenched again and my efforts to prevent the exploits of this "H_2O (dihydrogen monoxide) demon" are fruitless. I am at her mercy. Again, the audible gasp, including some other patrons in the restaurant. Also, there are some snickers. Our poor waitress (and I'm not referring to her abilities as a food server but to her feelings) is mortified. We all are embarrassed for her and try to assure her that we, especially myself, are not offended.

Again, the mop-up takes place. My lap is starting to feel somewhat cool by now. Our very distraught and visibly nervous waitress brings a third glass of ice water and sets it very carefully in front of me, but not too close. She reminds me of a wide receiver in football who, when attempting to catch a pass from the quarterback, takes his eyes off the ball to look downfield before the ball arrives. He drops the ball for an incomplete pass. My waitress (notice how she's "my waitress") must have taken her eyes off the glass because she "drops the pass," and a *third* glass of water is spilled all over me!

This time, everyone laughs. I mean, all of us laugh vigorously and with great enthusiasm. We aren't laughing at my waitress at her expense; it's just that the whole situation is comical. My waitress, though, doesn't think it's funny and rushes off to hide in the kitchen. Again, the cleanup routine, this time by the manager himself. Lawson quietly says to us, "She's in the back room crying. I'm going to make her come back and finish serving you." Oh, joy!

Eventually, my waitress returns. Her face is tear-streaked, and her hand visibly shakes as she attempts to place a *fourth* glass of ice water in front of me. I reach out and take her hand in both of mine, and together we guide the glass for a safe landing. In the background, I swear I could hear strains of Handel's "Hallelujah" chorus. Evidently, the third time was the charm. "In the name of the Father, the Son, and the Holy Spirit. Amen."

Wade in the Water
Wade in the water,
wade in the water, children,
wade in water
God's a-going to trouble the water.
WORDS: Afro-American spiritual

2

Wo Fat (Khigh Dheigh)

I RECENTLY WATCHED AN OLD MOVIE on television that reminded me of an incident that occurred to me some thirty-three years ago. The film was "The Manchurian Candidate," a 1962 American Cold War suspense thriller directed by John Frankenheimer from a screenplay by George Axelrod based on Richard Condon's 1959 novel. It starred Laurence Harvey, Frank Sinatra, and Janet Leigh and featured Angela Lansbury, Henry Silva, and James Gregory. All of these were Hollywood stars of yesteryear, and most are no longer living.

The film's central concept is that the son of a prominent right-wing political family is the victim of brainwashing. During his imprisonment as a P.O.W. in Korea, he is groomed for being an unwitting assassin for an international Communist conspiracy. First released at the height of the Cuban Missile Crisis on October 24, 1962, the film was a hit. It gained nominations for two Academy Awards.

One of the actors who had a minor role in the film was Khigh Dheigh. He is an American-born man who, despite looking sufficiently Asian for the part, was of mixed Anglo, Egyptian, and Sudanese ancestry. Dheigh played the part of Dr. Yen Lo, the devious Red Chinese doctor who hypnotizes the main character and controls his mind. Years later, this actor would play the role of Wo Fat, head of the Chinese mafia, on the CBS television series "Hawaii Five-O." He would be the arch-nemesis of Steve McGarrett, played by Jack Lord, the head of Hawaii's state police force.

While serving as pastor at the Chandler UMC from 1978-84, it was my privilege to have as one of our members the Postmaster of Chandler, Arizona. Fred had served in this capacity since 1959, first as Acting Postmaster, and then his position with the U.S. Postal Service became permanent a year later. Fred was a very articulate person, deeply committed to his Christian faith, and a loyal and respected member of the church. Then in 1980, Fred retired and invited Martha and me to his retirement dinner.

Fred asked me to give the blessing before eating our catered meal. Seated right next to me was a man that Fred had known for several years, a man who lived in Chandler at the time, the actor Khigh Dheigh. I was surprised!

I have since forgotten how Fred and Khigh Dheigh developed their friendship. I remember that it had progressed over the years, was genuine, and one full of respect and warmth for each other. I felt honored and humbled even to have a part in the evening's agenda. Little did I know how humbled I would be before the night was over.

During our meal, in conversation with this television actor, I attempted to make small talk. Awkwardly, turning on the charm and smiling my biggest grin, I said, "Mr. Dheigh, I have seen you in several episodes of 'Hawaii Five-O' and enjoy the program immensely."

Khigh Dheigh looked at me with a startled and curious look. Then he replied disdainfully, "I would hope that a person such as you would spend his time more wisely. The program is not for thinking persons."

I grew warm and felt my face turn red. I was embarrassed and humiliated. My effort to engage in polite conversation, even though it was "chitchat," was rebuffed. I didn't remember much of any further conversation after this brief exchange. I suppose some have the stereotype that ministers live in an ecclesiastical tower remote from real life. Perhaps they think we don't engage in anything trivial or mundane like reading novels, going to the movies, watching ballgames, telling jokes, enjoying Disneyland with their kids, or watching mind-numbing television shows such as "Hawaii Five-O." We, too, need to have a means of escape now and then. Sorry, Mr. Dheigh, old buddy. However, you should know that it's millions of people like me, who have provided the financial means you have enjoyed during your lifetime of acting.

James D. Wood

Make Me a Captive, Lord

Make me a captive, Lord, and then I shall be free.
Force me to render up my sword, and I shall conqueror be.
I sink in life's alarms when by myself I stand;
imprison me within thine arms, and strong shall be my hand.

WORDS: George Matheson, 1890 (Eph. 3:1)

3

Pleasure Cruise

WELL, I SUPPOSE MOST CRUISES are for pleasure. However, when I finished my active duty obligation with the U.S. Navy, I was required to complete my status in the reserves by participating in a couple of "two-week cruises." They took place during the summers of 1960 and 1961. These cruises, the first aboard a repair ship and the second on an aircraft carrier, were not altogether pleasurable.

Nevertheless, Martha and I took our first real pleasure cruise sometime... Hmm, when was it? Gosh, I can't remember when. Usually, my memory about such pivotal moments is not bad, but for the life of me, I just can't remember when this event occurred. Of course, it was during the summer, our children were no longer at home, so I'm going to guess that it during my appointment to Velda Rose UMC from 1984-89.

Regardless, it was a relatively short cruise, four days and three nights, from Los Angeles to Catalina Island (twenty-six miles across the sea) to Ensenada, Mexico, and back to Los Angeles. It would be on one of the Carnival Cruise line ships. I remember Martha coming home from work one day and announcing that she had heard of this fantastic deal—five hundred dollars for two persons. It sounded good to me, too, and a short cruise would give us some familiarity for any future excursions. We made the arrangements.

Though my memory is hazy regarding this cruise, I'm sure we elected for an inside cabin. It would be less expensive and, after all, who needs a view from a porthole when sleeping. We had the same table for breakfast and dinner meals. The same eight persons were our meal companions, and

I recall one elderly couple who seemed to book one cruise after another. Apparently, they had the financial resources, and it got a little tiresome hearing them compare one journey with another, especially hearing all their complaints. I surmised that they were unhappy and bored with life.

Lunchtime was different though. It was a buffet line where, when your food tray was complete, we would fill up one table, then the next, and so forth. We sat with different persons each day, and this variety of lunch companions and the ensuing conversation was a pleasant change.

One day during lunch, after we had departed Catalina Island, we struck up a conversation with a couple from Pennsylvania. They were both high school teachers, and during our discussion one of them asked, "Jim, what is it you do for a living?"

Over the years I have discovered that this question can be a conversation stopper. For when I respond, "I'm a minister," a sheet of ice drops between us. The questioner and his or her spouse have a perplexed look on their face, and I can almost read their minds, *Oh gosh, did I use any inappropriate words? I was getting ready to share a dirty joke. Oh, my. What a mistake that would have been.* And so on and so on. At least, that's what their facial expressions seem to indicate.

However, in this case, the sheet of ice never developed. The woman who asked the question responded with a smile saying, "You know, Jim, you seem like a minister." She continued by relating that she and her husband were followers of Jesus and part of a community of faith back home. Our conversation continued with spirit and enthusiasm long after the period designated for lunch. When we departed, we did so feeling that we had developed a new friendship. It was nice.

That evening, following another dinner with our usual table of eight and after hearing more complaints from our veteran cruisers, Martha and I strolled around the deck. It was a beautiful night, our time aboard the ship was ending, and we were enjoying the whole experience of cruising. U.S. regulations for cruise liners prohibit the operation of casinos between two American ports, for example between Los Angeles and Catalina Island. However, between an American port and foreign port casinos are legal to operate. At present, we were traveling between Catalina Island and Ensenada, Mexico. As we strolled about the main deck, we passed the ship's casino where games of chance, a less offensive euphemism for gambling, were taking place. I said to Martha, "I think I'll go in there and play a little Black Jack." She commented, "I'll just watch," meaning, *I'll see to it that you don't lose too much money.*

Blackjack or Twenty-one is the only game of chance I understand. I can count up to twenty-one, determine when to add another card or hold what I have without going over twenty-one. Easy, huh? I don't know the other intricacies of the game, though, and I'm not interested in them. I'm not compulsive with this game, having played it less than six times in my life. I have always quit when I've lost twenty dollars or when Martha squeezes hard on my arm. Then I get the message that it's time to fold up and leave.

So, I saunter into the casino with Martha trailing me. At the blackjack table, I see the man with whom we had had a delightful lunch conversation. I ask him, "Do you mind if I join you?"

If the man is surprised to see me, he doesn't show it. "Jim! Yes, please join me. I'm just getting started." I notice that his wife is not present as he greets Martha. We begin playing in earnest and, after five minutes and a loss of ten dollars, then the man's wife enters the casino. She apparently knows the table where her husband is playing because she immediately heads our way. She also sees me with her husband. From across the room, she yells, "Oh, hi Reverend Wood!"

Time suddenly stops. The cards the dealer is passing stop in mid-air. Somebody turned down the volume of sound. Everything is quiet. The silence is deafening. No one moves. The room becomes dark, and a spotlight appears out of nowhere shining directly on me. Everyone is staring. For what seemed like ten seconds or more, then the cards fall on the table; the sound comes up again; there is movement once more, and conversation returns to the casino. More than anything, I notice that Martha isn't squeezing my arm tight anymore. Moreover, I can breathe again as my heartbeat returns to normal.

I don't remember much after that. I know I reached my twenty-dollar loss limit because Martha informed me of this fact. We said our goodbyes to the couple and unsteadily walked out of the casino. When we reached the passageway, Martha exclaimed through gritted teeth, "I could have killed that woman!" Have I shared with you that my wife can be very intense at times?

That's it. That's what I remember about our first pleasure cruise. Apparently, I have blocked out some memories connected with this trip.

Stand By Me

When the storms of life are raging, stand by me;
when the storms of life are raging, stand by me;
When the world is tossing me, like a ship upon the sea,
thou who rulest wind and water, stand by me.

WORDS: Charles A. Tindley, ca. 1906 (Mt. 8:23-
27; Mk. 4:35-41; Lk. 8:22-25)

4

Internal Revenue Service

WHILE SERVING AS A PART-TIME STUDENT PASTOR in seminary from 1968-71, I received the grand salary of $4,000 per year. Furnished by the small congregation I served—John Collins UMC—were our housing and utilities. At that time the Social Security Administration considered pastors, regardless of full or part-time, as "self-employed." In my past employment with the City of San Diego and the Port District of San Diego, my employers always paid part of my Social Security while deducting from my salary another portion. Now I was expected to contribute the entire amount myself.

My income was small and limited. I was supporting a wife and two children and had school expenses, mostly the cost of textbooks, on top of everything else. I commiserated all this to a fellow student one day, and he said, "Jim, you can file for an exemption and not pay Social Security. Ministers are eligible for this allowance." Really? Sounded good to me as more than half of my annual salary could be used for living expenses. I filed and received the exemption Form 4361 from the Social Security Administration. Problem solved, at least for several years.

Twenty-two years later, while serving the church I began in Gold Canyon, just south of Apache Junction, Arizona, I received a letter from the Internal Revenue Service. It informed me that I had failed to pay Social Security for the past several years and unless I could provide them with a copy of my exemption, I was in arrears and would have to come up with several thousand dollars that included interest. With my mind reeling, I tried to remember where I had filed my Form 4361. I no longer had copies of my income tax returns from my earlier seminary years. I thought that perhaps I had stapled the exemption form to one of those returns and had, subsequently, destroyed it. I was in trouble.

We were still using an income tax firm from Long Beach, California where I served my first appointment. I called them and asked if they had kept copies of my returns during those years. My agent stated that he and his partner had split up, and each had half the files. He would check and get back to me.

Meanwhile, since I had not responded to IRS, they continued to send letters that became more threatening with each mailing. My agent in Long Beach eventually called back and informed me that he could not find a copy of Form 4361. He stated that he thought that IRS was playing a "dirty trick," attempting to get me to start paying Social Security again. Before enrolling in seminary, I had worked in the public sector (including my time in the U.S. Navy) and had accumulated the necessary forty-quarters (ten years) needed to qualify for Social Security benefits. My agent said that it was up to me. "You could get back on board with Social Security, and you will have greater benefits if you so choose this route."

I didn't like the idea that IRS was attempting coercive methods, and my stubbornness ruled the day. A year passed, and I continued to receive more letters from the IRS, each more menacing. Then I received an appointment to a congregation in Phoenix—Cross Roads UMC. One of the members of this church worked for the IRS, and I shared with her my problem. She explored the claim by the IRS but could offer no solution. It looked like I would have to take out a loan and repay Social Security for the missing years.

Then, unexpectedly, I received a telephone call from my former agent in Long Beach (I was presently working with another tax preparer). "Guess what I just received from Social Security in Sacramento, California?" he asked. Before I could respond, he continued, "A copy of your exemption Form 4361."

I was astounded! I couldn't believe it (though why would I doubt God's handling of this problem). My former agent said, "I'm faxing it to your church office, and I suggest that you make several copies and keep them in your safety deposit box or some other secure place." I thanked him and breathed a deep sigh of relief and gratitude.

I printed several copies of the long-lost form, wrote a letter to IRS stating that I finally secured a duplicate they had requested and hoped this would be the end of our correspondence. Months passed without a reply from this intimidating governmental agency. Finally, a letter from them arrived in the mail. I anxiously tore open the envelope and read, "We have been reviewing your past tax returns and found that you have paid us more than $1,000.00. Enclosed is our check to you for this amount." As the Russian comedian, Yakov Smirnoff often says, "What a country!"

God Will Take Care of You

Be not dismayed whate'er the tide, God will take care of you;
beneath his wings of love abide, God will take care of you.
God will take care of you, through every day, o'er all the way;
he will take care of you, God will take care of you.

WORDS: Civilla D. Martin, 1904

5

Jury Duty

THROUGHOUT MY MINISTRY, I have had the privilege of being asked to serve, as part of my responsibility as a U.S. citizen, on a jury. Now that I have reached a certain age, I am no longer required to serve in this capacity.

Sometime during my appointment to the Cross Roads UMC in Phoenix (1992-98), I received a summons to report for jury duty at the Municipal Courthouse in Phoenix. To my amazement, my name was called to sit in the jury box for questioning by the lawyers representing the case. The case involved a suit by an elderly woman, against the defendant, one of the large chain stores in our area.

The woman was doing some shopping at this store and slipped in a puddle of spilled beverage on the floor, shattering both of her hips. She is suing the store for medical bills and emotional compensation.

Before questioning prospective jurors by the attorneys, the judge asked if any of us had a reason we could not serve on the jury. Hesitantly, I raise my hand. The judge seems annoyed and consults the seating list of those sitting in the jury box. "Yes, Reverend Wood. Your reason?"

"Your honor (I make sure to treat him with judicial respect), I have several persons undergoing life crises at this time. Some are hospitalized, and others are in the process of dying. As their pastor, I need to be available for their needs." It's the truth, but the judge is not sympathetic.

"Let me ask this, Reverend Wood. What arrangements do you make for the needs of your congregation when you go on vacation?"

I can see where this is going and answer timidly, "I ask a colleague to cover for me."

The judge (with a slight grin on his face) responds, "Right. Not excused."

The attorneys for the plaintiff and defendant agree and nod their heads. I will be in for the duration. The judge excuses the sitting jury, telling us that the trial is set to begin tomorrow morning.

The next day, the plaintiff's lawyer presents the background for his client's suit against the store. The damage caused by her fall is extensive and medically expensive. The store was negligent in not cleaning up the spill after it occurred. Nothing is said concerning monetary compensation. This will be up to the jury to decide.

The argument by the defendant's lawyers (notice the plural) is strange. Their primary defense is that the store has a policy regarding spills and cleanups. When one occurs, an employee is required to "stand guard" over the spill or bring a shopping cart to place over the liquid while he or she gets some paper towels. In fact, their stores have paper towels at each checkout stand for this purpose as well as paper towel dispensers on individual columns throughout the store.

This policy makes sense to me, and it sounds like a good one, but I wonder, *Why were the employees slow in responding to the spill?* This whole scenario of arguments for both sides takes most of the morning. During the lunch break, I write two questions for the judge. One: "Is it possible for a juror to ask a question of the lawyers." Two: "If so, then where was the closest column pole to the spill area with a paper towel dispenser?" I submit my written questions to one of the bailiffs.

After lunch, we reconvene and once again sit in the jury box; the judge states that he has a question from one of the jurors. "Yes, jurors can ask written questions of the lawyers." Then he relates my other question to them. The attorney for the store asks the manager to make use of a diagram of the store and to point out the nearest paper towel dispenser. The manager points to a location not five feet away from where the accident occurred. The lawyer for the plaintiff immediately sees the intent of my question. Smiling, he asks the manager where the employee went to get the paper towels for wiping up the spill. Reluctantly, the manager points to one of the checkout stands, some twenty-five feet further away. Case closed.

We, the jury, awarded the woman $500,000 in damages. She will never be able to walk correctly again and without pain. I thought it was fair compensation. I discovered, afterward, that each store is separate from the corporation, a franchise if you will, and this prohibits any suit against the larger one. The half million dollars would come from this one store. Also, I discovered the primary attorney for the store was a member of a neighboring United Methodist Church. He asked me if his office could contact me in a few days for a brief survey. I agreed to his request.

Since this time, though I have been called to serve on several occasions, I have not been seated again. Nevertheless, it was an interesting, enlightening, and worthwhile experience. I would recommend it to anyone.

Just as I Am, Without One Plea

Just as I am, without one plea,
but that thy blood was shed for me,
and that thou bidst me come to thee,
O Lamb of God, I come, I come.

WORDS: Charlotte Elliott, 1835

6

An Amtrak Vacation

SOMETIME IN THE SUMMER OF 2000, during our time at Willowbrook UMC, Martha and I made vacation plans to visit Walt Disney World in Orlando, Florida. We always lived close to Disneyland, the original theme park that opened in 1955 in Anaheim, California, and visited it many times. First, we enjoyed it with our children when they were younger. Now, in recent years, we saw the same excitement in the faces of some of our grandchildren. Though we were close to retirement, we looked forward to experiencing Disney's newer and larger theme park.

To arrive at our destination, we elected to travel by rail to Orlando on Amtrak. The National Railroad Passenger Corporation, doing business as Amtrak, is a publicly funded service operated and managed as a for-profit corporation. It began operations on May 1, 1971, to provide intercity passenger service in the United States. The name Amtrak is a combination of the words "America" and "trak," the latter itself an inventive spelling of "track."

We chose the route called the "Sunset Limited," and would have to depart from the station in Tucson, as there was none in Phoenix. However, our one-way passenger tickets (we would fly back home) did include a Greyhound Bus ride from Phoenix to Tucson. We were not aware, or perhaps did not read the instructions carefully, that there were two bus pickup points in Phoenix. We went to the wrong one.

Our adventurous trip began on a Friday morning. Our next-door neighbors drove us to the central Greyhound Bus station. Logical thinking, right? Only when we presented our tickets to the attendant behind the counter, he looked puzzled. We informed him of our Amtrak passenger plan, including the need for transportation to Tucson via bus, and he still didn't comprehend our tickets and their schedule. Finally, he stated, "Well, our plan doesn't match your reservation number. Nevertheless, we have a bus you can ride. It leaves in twenty minutes."

By the time the bus departed Phoenix thirty-five minutes later, we felt stressed and somewhat uncomfortable. When we finally reached Tucson, having to take another mode of transportation to the train station, we discovered that our Amtrak train had already left—five minutes earlier!

Well, what to do? I asked the stationmaster when the next Sunset Limited train would arrive. "Next Monday," was his reply.

With a sinking feeling, I asked what our possibilities might be to accomplish our travel plans.

He suggested that we take a taxi to the airport and catch a flight to San Antonio, Texas. "Tomorrow morning, at six o'clock, the train is scheduled to arrive at the station."

I considered this for a moment and then asked, "It sounds as if we're going to attain some additional expenses. Would Amtrak reimburse us for these extra costs?"

He replied, "Well, keep receipts of your expenses and file a claim with our main headquarters. I can't say whether or not you'll get the entire amount back, but it wouldn't hurt to try."

We quickly caught a taxi to the airport and were able to purchase one-way tickets to San Antonio. The price was outrageous, but we held hope for reimbursement. After a two-hour plane ride, we finally arrived in San Antonio in the mid-afternoon. Then another taxi trip to a Red Roof Inn that was within short walking distance of the train station. Two taxi rides, two plane tickets, and now the cost of overnight motel accommodations (plus meals incurred during this scramble)—the out-of-pocket expenses were piling up. To shorten the story, we were able to catch the train the next morning. Of course, it would be two hours late! The only rail station, on our entire trip, where the train was on time was Tucson.

We enjoyed a hearty and delicious breakfast aboard the train. Our compartment was small but comfortable. From San Antonio, we would travel to Houston and then on to New Orleans. We enjoyed most of the scenery but were tired and weary from the worry and pressure of trying to make alternate arrangements. We looked forward to a night's sleep.

Our compartment had one small bed. Another hammock-type bed hung on straps above it. Martha quickly opted for the lower, more comfortable arrangement, while I reluctantly agreed to sleep in the upper bunk. I soon discovered two things. One, you better not be claustrophobic because it was a tight fit. Two, you better have iron kidneys because if in the middle of the night, you needed to make a trip to use the toilet facilities, it was going to take a while. Our Amtrak vacation was beginning to lose some of its luster.

Once we reached New Orleans, the trip took a decidedly downward turn. There was no scenery. It appeared as if we were traveling through a green tunnel. Vegetation was overgrown on both sides of the railroad track so that we could not see anything beyond it. We went through the southern part of Mississippi and Alabama and on into Florida. Several times the train stopped, and we would be relegated to a sidetrack. Sometimes sitting for hours, we inquired and discovered that the reason was a freight train. It seems that this was where Amtrak made its money (remember the "for-profit" angle?) and gave the trains carrying freight priority over passengers. "Strike two!"

Finally, we arrived at a small community south of Jacksonville, Florida. The tracks from there to Orlando were washed out from a recent rainstorm. We would be transferred to a bus for transportation to the train station at our final destination. This schedule change would add more hours of delay, and by the time we reached our hotel it was past midnight, and we were late almost eight hours. "Strike three, you're out!"

Nevertheless, we enjoyed Walt Disney World. It was very humid in Orlando, and we felt as if we had emerged from a sauna fully clothed. We were able to visit Cape Kennedy (formerly Cape Canaveral) where NASA launched human-crewed flights into space. However, we were glad that our return trip home was by plane.

Postscript: I compiled our list of expenses, made copies of our receipts, and submitted everything, including the unclear instructions for bus pickup in Phoenix, to Amtrak. The total was over $1,800. Months later, Amtrak responded. "Sorry for the misunderstanding. Though we cannot reimburse your extra expenses; nevertheless, we are happy to include a $1,000 voucher for your next Amtrak adventure." Hmmm. You can bet we'll use it!

It's Me, It's Me, O Lord

It's me (it's me), it's me, O Lord, standing in the need of prayer.
It's me (it's me), it's me, O Lord, standing in the need of prayer.
Not my brother, not my sister, but it's me, O Lord,
standing in the need of prayer.
Not my brother, not my sister, but it's me, O Lord,
standing in the need of prayer.

WORDS: Afro-American spiritual

7

Another Amtrak Experience

IN THE SUMMER OF 2002, I took a three-month study leave, spending most of it in England. In my memoir, I describe our adventures in this beautiful country through a church exchange with an English Methodist pastor, the Reverend Alan Coustick. Following our return home, and as part of our itinerary plan, we visited one of our church members who spends her summers in Kent, Washington. To accomplish this, we decided to use our Amtrak voucher, traveling by train from San Diego to Tacoma, staying four or five days with our friend, and returning to San Diego by a jetliner. Another Amtrak journey. Were we out of our minds? Maybe, but somehow and sometime we had to take advantage of the voucher's value.

We started our trip in mid-September. My parents, who live in the San Diego area, were celebrating their sixty-fifth wedding anniversary. Although it was a joyous and happy occasion and most of the Wood family was present, the festivities were somewhat subdued. My mother, suffering more and more from the ravages of dementia, would be placed in a care center following the party.

We left our vehicle with family, and the next day boarded the Amtrak train for Tacoma. The route along the Pacific Ocean to Los Angeles was beautiful to view. Surfers rode the ocean waves, and small communities dotted the coastline. From Los Angeles to San Francisco, the train headed inland away from the ocean. Though the landscape became increasing brown (remember California is the "Golden State"); nevertheless, the scenery was still pleasant to the eye. We had planned, before making our reservations, to leave the train in Oakland, travel by taxi to San Francisco, and spend a couple of nights at a hotel near the Fisherman's Wharf area. Amtrak graciously allowed us to make this diversion. After a time of exploring the city through a cable and streetcar tour, eating delicious food at some great restaurants, and visiting Alcatraz, we boarded a different train to resume our journey.

Again, we had similar sleeping arrangements, good food for our meals, and the same delays for the freight train priority. We were supposed to arrive in Tacoma around seven o'clock in the evening, but when that time came; we were far from our destination. Since the schedule indicated we would be in Tacoma, the train stewards refused to make up our compartment for sleeping. I chose, instead of sleeping in the upper bunk, to find an empty, available compartment for the night. I discovered one close by, said, "Good-night" to Martha, put my wallet on the nightstand, and turned in for what I hoped would be a sound sleep.

We arrived in Tacoma early the next morning, twelve hours late. Martha yelled, "Jim, we're here!" I quickly got dressed, got our luggage together, got off the train, and met our host who was a little anxious that she had to make two trips to pick us up. She had not called Amtrak to determine the train's on-time schedule. About halfway to her home, in a wave of panic, I shouted, "I left my wallet on the train!"

We turned around and went back to the station. The train was still there, and I got permission to re-board and look for my wallet. I found the compartment I had slept in, but it was clean, leaving no trace of my belongings. I asked the steward who was present if he had seen my wallet. He sympathetically shook his head. Fortunately, Martha had our return flight tickets in her possession, and when we got to the home of our host, I made some calls canceling our credit cards and my driver's license. I would have no personal photo ID for boarding our plane when we left in a few days.

I called our oldest daughter, who has access to our safety deposit box, and asked her to obtain my passport and mail it to me at our host's address. It was delivered a few hours before we were to board the plane on our return flight to San Diego. Whew!

Another postscript: Since my driver's license was in my missing wallet, Martha would have to drive home from San Diego. Just outside of El Centro on the way to Yuma, I noticed Martha dozing off at the wheel of our automobile. "Pullover," I cried. I drove the rest of the way home, license or not. I now do all our road trip driving. Nevertheless, no more Amtrak train trips!

He Leadeth Me: O Blessed Thought

He leadeth me: O blessed thought!
O words with heavenly comfort fraught!
What e'er I do, where'er I be, 'tis God's hand that leadeth me.
He leadeth me, he leadeth me, by his own hand he leadeth me;
his faithful follower I would be, for by his hand he leadeth me.

WORDS: Joseph H. Gilmore, 1862 (Ps. 23)

8

The Mortician

WHILE SERVING AS A RETIRED associate pastor at Sun Lakes UMC, from 2004-09, Martha and I made financial arrangements for a couple of niches in the courtyard area of the church's property called The Gardens. The Gardens is a quiet, tranquil, sacred area that proposes a "final resting place" for members of its community of faith. Three choices are offered: 1) a single or double-niche large enough to contain cremated ashes, 2) a spot in the ground where ashes can be buried without identifying markers or 3) a separate vault area where memorial plaques can be placed to honor deceased family members. The area devoted to these purposes is also known as "The Columbarium."

One day, after being under appointment to the church for about three years, the office manager told me that she had a proposition. It seems that another couple, with the same last name as ours, was moving to another state to be closer to their children. They had already engraved a nameplate with their name WOOD but would not be using it. Would we want to purchase it for our niches at a cut-rate price? I know a bargain when I see it, and quickly accepted the deal without consulting Martha. She is better qualified and well known in our family for sniffing out bargains, but she beamed when I told her of the offer.

Shortly after that, I happened to walk through the courtyard area on my way to the church's fellowship hall. I noticed one of the men on The Gardens committee doing some work. It surprised me to see that he was installing this newly acquired nameplate on our niche. This particular man had retired from the mortuary business before moving to Arizona. I casually said, "Hey, Don. That's our nameplate you're installing."

He smiled and replied, "I know."

Continuing the conversation, I inquired, "Will you and your wife have your ashes placed here?"

He shrugged and replied, "Well, no. You see, Jim, we were both married to other persons. Her husband died, and my wife died. We knew each other socially and eventually got married. However, we both have burial plots back in our home state."

I couldn't resist saying, "Well, Don, as you know, with cremation you could have your ashes both here and there."

Don nodded his head in agreement and said, "Yes, I know. However, we've already arranged for our coffins and have purchased burial plots. Our families expect us to honor this arrangement."

It will come as no surprise, for those who know me best, to discover how I responded: "Don, you were a mortician before you retired, right? You know as well as I do that when viewing a person's body in the casket, the only part showing is from the waist up."

Don's face went from a shocked expression to a wide grin as he realized what I was intimating. Then he broke into hearty laughter, and I joined him.

Please understand that I'm not making light of death's reality. It's part of the human condition, of life, that we are all finite creatures, and we will all experience death in one form or another. Some, more than others, are exposed daily to its reality. Those engaged in military combat and law enforcement, surgeons and nurses, firefighters and EMT personnel—all these persons are quite familiar with the ways death makes its appearance and its resulting aftermath. Morticians and ministers too. I have certainly seen my share.

As a person of faith, though, I have a different perspective. I accept death as inevitable, but not something to be feared. Everyone experiences death differently. Some deaths are shocking, tragic, devastating, and heart-rending. The accompanying grief for the survivors is substantial, hurtful, and long-lasting. Other deaths, especially to the elderly, seem to bring peace and an end to suffering, a well-deserved rest after enduring the indignities and insults associated with growing older. Those who have achieved a lifespan of "four score and seven years" know this to be true.

Nevertheless, the prospect of my death does not have the power to frighten me. If I can trust God with my living, day by day by day, then why should I not trust God with my dying and death? "There is no fear in love, but perfect love casts out fear; for fear has to do with punishment, and whoever fears has not reached perfection in love." (1 John 4:18). I think the retired mortician understood this, too.

I'll Praise My Maker While I've Breath

I'll praise my Maker while I've breath; and
when my voice is lost in death,
praise shall employ my nobler powers.
My days of praise shall ne'er be past, while life, and thought,
and being last, or immortality endures.
WORDS: Isaac Watts, 1719; alt. by John Wesley, 1737 (Ps. 146)

9

South African Krugerrand

THE QUESTION REGARDING GIFTS to pastors and parsonage families has always plagued ministers. Specifically, the question of how to avoid the pitfalls around them more than about how to encourage or secure them. There are those gifts that are not gifted at all. In many of our churches, the Trustees or Staff-Parish Relations Committee sets a fee or an honorarium for weddings or memorial services. This fee, not a gift, and by whatever name you call it, it is taxable income. In reading the *Book of Discipline*, a guideline for those in The United Methodist Church, it is my understanding that the minister is not to accept a fee for the above services if the family or persons are members of his or her community of faith. Apparently, some of my colleagues do not have the same understanding.

All of this is a prelude to my having received a gift sometime during the latter part of my appointment to Crossroads UMC, 1992-98. I became acquainted with a couple, members of the church, who were going through a difficult life situation. Carolyn and her husband lived in one of those retirement homes that include an adjacent healthcare facility. Her husband was very ill and had been confined primarily to his room in this facility. He would eat his meals in the dining room with the other patients but was not able to participate in group activities and had little human contact other than with his nurses and wife. I would make a point to call upon him once a month. Carolyn asked me to notify her when I scheduled my visits so she could be present, too.

After a couple of years of visitation, Carolyn's husband died. I was asked to have his memorial service and gladly agreed. I continued to visit

Carolyn on the same time basis, giving spiritual support and pastoral care. Then, in the spring of 1998, I announced to the congregation that Martha and I would be leaving them for a new appointment to a church in Sun City.

When Carolyn received word of our leaving, she called me and requested a last visit. These visits are always tough for the pastor and parishioner alike. Together, we recall the love and respect we have for one another. We shed tears, remembering sad times shared. Laughter comes forth as we remember the good and fun times. We did this, and when it came time to depart, Carolyn said, "Reverend Jim, I want you to have something, a gift from me to you." I was hesitant as she retrieved a small box that previously held some jewelry, perhaps a diamond ring. When I reluctantly opened it, I saw that it contained a gold coin. Upon further inspection, I noticed it was a South African gold Krugerrand. It took me by complete surprise.

"Oh, Carolyn," I said. "I can't accept this; it's not proper. What I've done for you and your husband was done out of love and concern for you both. It's what I've been called to do as your pastor."

Carolyn was insistent. She explained that she and her husband had invested in several of these coins at a time when they were worth $1,000 an ounce, the weight of each coin. Now the price of gold had dropped to less than $200 per ounce. I would honor her if I accepted this gift, perhaps waiting until the price of gold rose again, and then use it for some worthwhile mission project.

I gave it some thought and with some reservation replied, "Alright. With that stipulation, I will gladly accept your generous gift." Carolyn's face beamed, and tears came to her eyes. I knew I had made the right decision.

I placed the case with the gold coin in our safety deposit box, and there it stayed for more than ten years. Then in 2008, while living in Sun Lakes after retirement, our annual conference, The Desert Southwest Conference, announced a particular fund drive. The primary emphasis would financially underwrite the start of new congregations. Moreover, a secondary part of this financial focus would allow persons to give additional funds supporting the work of Africa University. Africa University is a private, Pan-African and United Methodist-related educational institution.

It has more than 1,200 students from twenty-two African countries. Its location is near Mutare, Zimbabwe's fourth largest city. It grants both Bachelor's and Master's degrees in various programs. What better use for this Krugerrand coin, a coin minted in a country known for its earlier apartheid policy regarding its black compatriots? Now was the time to use Carolyn's gift.

After discussing my thought with Martha, I contacted our district superintendent and told her of our intentions. The price of gold had increased to a little over $1,000 an ounce, and we wanted whatever the converted amount to be forwarded to Africa University. Delighted with our idea of re-gifting our gift, she thanked us and indicated that she would direct our instructions to the conference treasurer.

A colleague writes, concerning the burning question of gifts:

> *If you would be reluctant to tell your mother or your brother, the IRS agent, or the chair of your Staff-Parish Relations Committee about the gift you received and who gave it, then I would suggest that you think twice about accepting it—no matter how generous or nice it is.*

Thank you, Carolyn, for your generous gift. I have not in the least been reluctant to write about how beautiful it was. It has helped some needy student somewhere in Africa. Who? Only God knows, and that's enough.

And Can It Be that I Should Gain

And can it be that I should gain
an interest in the Savior's blood?
Died he for me, who caused his pain?
For me, who him to death pursued?
Amazing love! how can it be
That thou my Lord,
shouldst die for me?
Amazing love! how can it be
That thou, my Lord,
shouldst die for me?

WORDS: Charles Wesley, 1739 (Acts 16:26)

10

Diagnosis: Cancer

IN MY MEMOIR, THE CHAPTER ENTITLED, "Freedom to Travel More," I briefly wrote about our personal health and the fact that Martha and I have had very few problems with which to deal. I spoke too soon. That is, I wrote too early.

I finished writing my book in December of 2011, and it became available for distribution after publication in November of 2012. However, previously, in January 2012, I was scheduled for my bi-annual dermatology examination. Growing up in the San Diego area, I frequented the beaches each summer getting sunburn after sunburn to get a healthy-looking tan. Consequently, I have become prone to pre-cancerous spots, especially on my scalp, that require the burning off with liquid nitrogen. I have also had several biopsies conducted on other parts of my body that proved to be negative.

However, at this appointment, I asked the doctor about a small lump on the left side of my back. I had noticed it, located just below my shoulder blade and above the hip area, several months previously. Though it didn't concern me, I was curious as to what it might be. After a routine examination, the doctor said, "Oh, that's just fatty tissue, very common, nothing to worry about though."

Not entirely satisfied with her response, I asked if it would grow larger.

"Maybe, and if it does, you can have it surgically removed. But I wouldn't do anything at this point." Her diagnosis and subsequent prognosis satisfied me, somewhat.

A month later, I had an appointment with my primary care physician. It was a routine examination that followed some blood work that I had done. Upon completion, my doctor asked, "Any other concerns?" I mentioned the lump on my back, and she felt and probed it. "Oh, that's just fatty tissue, very common, nothing to worry about though." Hey, did these two medical professionals attend the same school?

I wanted to know more, so I asked, "What if it doesn't stay the same size but grows larger?"

"Well," she began to explain, "If you have it removed now it will require an incision about two inches long. However, if fatty tissue grows larger, it may need an incision about six inches long."

I replied, "Why would I want one this long (measuring with my thumb and index finger), when I could have one (again measuring) this long?"

Looking at me intently, she suggested, "If you want, I can refer you to a general surgeon." I asked for the referral.

A week or so later, I met with a cancer specialist. You wouldn't believe his response after he examined me. "Oh, that's just fatty tissue, very common, nothing to worry about though." I insisted on its removal and made an appointment for its accomplishment the next week.

During the surgery (the area being localized with a numbing agent) the doctor commented, "Oh, this is a little deeper than I thought. Nevertheless, we'll send it for analyzing and let you know the results in a week. Still, I don't think there's anything for you to worry about." Ha!

The following week when I met with the doctor for the lab results, he seemed uneasy and somewhat hesitant. It almost pained him to tell me. "Mr. Wood, I'm sorry, but it is a form of cancer—myxofibrosarcoma. I'm going to refer you to a colleague for further treatment and surgery." I gulped and could almost feel the blood draining from my face.

Then a comforting peace from God settled into my being. I replied, "Alright, whatever it takes. I'm in good hands in more ways than one."

I was referred to an excellent surgeon. I would undergo a couple of MRIs, PT and CT scans, and twenty-five sessions of radiation. The radiation would reduce the size of cancer, thus making the area of the surgery smaller. The procedure itself took place near the end of July 2012. The operation was successful. Some removal of muscle in my back was necessary, but not much.

I have been on the giving side of many who have had surgical procedures and hospital stays. I have met with them before hospitalization, and we prayed together. At their home, before going in for surgery, following surgery, and after they had returned home—we prayed. Then I called to check with them as they proceeded with physical therapy and recuperation. Now I was on the receiving end of God's love through family, friends, and colleagues. I can't tell you how much this meant to me.

It's been more than six years since my surgery. My cancer has not returned, and I have been released from any further follow-ups. I thank God for the peace that God offers through Christ and the love given through those who genuinely care. I would also encourage you to listen to what your body tells you. Remember, it's called "the practice of medicine" for a reason.

Postscript: After sharing my experience with both my primary care physician and dermatologist about my subsequent surgery, they apologized. My primary care physician later told me that the surgeon to which she had initially referred contacted her. "Angela," he said, "you referred one of your patients to me who had a one in a million chance of having cancer (meaning me). Now you just referred me to another of your patients (a woman) who had a one in ten million chance of having cancer. What's going on? How did you become so skilled in detecting cancer in your patients?"

My doctor replied, "I started listening to my patients more." God does, indeed, work in mysterious ways!

There Is a Balm in Gilead
There is a balm in Gilead to make the wounded whole;
there is a balm in Gilead to heal the sin-sick soul.
Sometimes I feel discouraged, and think my work's in vain.
But then the Holy Spirit revives my soul again.
WORDS: Afro-American spiritual (Jer. 8:22)

11

Colloquialisms

COLLOQUIALISMS, AS MOST KNOW, are words, phrases, and expressions that come from everyday, informal speech. They encompass slang expressions but do not indicate poor or illiterate usage of language. With that in mind, I want to offer a word of explanation or my rationale for presenting this piece of writing.

When I was required to write term papers in high school, my English teacher, Mrs. Elizabeth Stone, would go ballistic if we used trite expressions in our presentations. Oops, sorry for the word ballistic, Mrs. Stone. This word, of course, was not part of our vocabulary at that time, as long-range ballistic missiles were not part of our military arsenal. However, I digress.

Trite expressions or cliché phrases, according to Webster, are those words "worn out by constant use; no longer having a freshness, originality, or novelty." Excluded from this genre would be colloquialisms for reasons already mentioned. Also eliminated to some degree but not entirely, are slang expressions. Some slang vocabulary has developed from an attempt to find fresh and vigorous, colorful, pungent, or humorous illustrations, and passes into disuse or comes to have a more formal status. However, some, with some modifications, carry over from generation to generation.

An interesting phenomenon developed in the 4th century. St. Jerome prepared a Latin version of the Bible, authorized by the Roman Catholic Church so that the people of that time could read it in a familiar, easily understood, language. This new version was called the Vulgate, derived from the word vulgar. It just means, "Characteristic of, belonging to, or common to the great mass of people in general; common; popular." Quite a difference from the root word, which implies crude, coarse, and unrefined.

Every generation, it seems, has cultivated its colloquialisms, idioms, slang, and trite expressions. Most were uniquely developed and used within that generation and, seldom if ever, crossed over to succeeding age groups who constructed their particular manifestations. Nevertheless, it appears to me that the generation following mine has taught their children well. They transmitted their unique vocabulary and even assimilated the slang expressions of their children so that the two generations are indistinguishable in their speech. There may be useful and valid reasons for this. Communicating in a standard language may be one. Another may be an attempt on the part of parents and others to relate to the world of their children, particularly when the child reaches adolescence. However, in some cases, it could be that the adult has never learned proper grammar usage. If she or he did, however, perhaps they were reluctant to demonstrate it for fear of being rejected by a society that appears bent on dumbing down our language.

Does this observation seem harsh? I can understand writers of fiction and non-fiction by applying common language to the characters they are developing. The printed page, whether it is newspapers, magazines or books, continues to present words in context and with, for the most part, proper usage of the English language. The same is not true of those who rely on verbal skills and the spoken word: television newscasters, sports commentators, personality interviewers, and even writers of fictional novels. Have you noticed the incorrect language structure, sentences ending with prepositions, wrong verb tenses, and conversation replete with trite expressions and current buzzwords? I do not want to sound like an intellectual snob or imitate a person who smugly acts superior about his particular tastes or interests. Nor do I feel that I have to impress others with my level of education and general command of the language. Those who know me best, know that is not who I am. However, it makes me sad to see those who should be aware of misusing and even abusing our language to be popular and "with it." Oops, sorry again, Mrs. Stone.

Okay, so with all this in mind, the following is an attempt at satire, a conversational caricature between a grandfather and his grandson. It doesn't mean to ridicule but rather to have fun. All names have been changed to protect the innocent, and any similarities to anyone living or dead are purely coincidental... ha! Here's the scene: Late Saturday morning, the telephone rings, and the grandfather answers:

"Start talkin' it's your nickel."

"Sup, dude. Oh, I mean ... sorry, Grandpa. Guess I forgot who I was calling."

"Alan! Hey, no sweat. What's happening?"

"Well, me'n my friend, that is, her and me are planning to take in the latest movie in 3D at the IMAX. I was wondering if you and grandma saw it and would like, you know, recommend it?"

"Are you kidding? I dig it, and you bet your sweet bippy we saw it. It was boss, a real gas, groovy. Nothing lame about it. Yeah; we'd give it two thumbs up!"

"Mad awesome! Now that's what I'm talking about. You guys are so cool!"

"Well, yeah, Alan. You know how hot it gets here during the summer, and we are keeping cool with our AC. But the AC in the IMAX was too cold, and grandma just about froze to death."

"Huh? Whatever. Anyway, Grandpa here's the thing... We definitely and absolutely want to hook up and hang out, but it costs a little more for 3D, and I'm maxed out until next Tuesday. So, I'm thinking do you suppose...?"

"Alan, I'm hip. You and that chick must be tight. Is she your main squeeze? Don't worry about it; I think I can spring for some extra bread, but you gotta pay it back. Otherwise, a knuckle sandwich..."

"Woo hoo! Shut the door! Grandpa, you're too much, 24/7 fer sure!"

"Well, Alan, you've significantly impacted my life, and so I'm just happy to help you out of an egregious situation."

"Huh? Oh, no problem, Grandpa, totally. Check it out. I'll, like, give you an update on our... Whatever."

"Unreal, but just remember to be proactive as you get transitioned into the Passion Pit. You are just going to see the flick, aren't you?"

"Say what? Oh, definitely. Chill out, Grandpa. We're not going clubbing or anything like that."

"Crazy. Have a blast but remember, Alan... Don't go ape and no back seat bingo!"

"Huh? Whatever. Sweet. Thanks, Grandpa. Nice talkin' to you, bless up."

"No sweat. You razz my berries. Later, gator."

Voice of Grandma: "That was Alan, I presume."

"Yep. Guess I'll head off to my man cave, watch some baseball on the idiot box, and maybe even catch a few zzzs. Neato, huh?"

I Stand Amazed in the Presence

I stand amazed in the presence of Jesus the Nazarene,
and wonder how he could love me, a sinner, condemned, unclean.
O how marvelous! O how wonderful! And my song shall ever be:
O how marvelous! O how wonderful! is my Savior's love for me!
WORDS: Charles H. Gabriel, 1905 (Lk. 22:41-44)

12

Legacy (a sermon)

WHAT FOLLOWS IS A SERMON preached on a Sunday morning preceding Veterans Day, 2012. It was also the twenty-fifth anniversary of the founding of Sun Lakes United Methodist Church. The title is "What Will They Say of Us?" and the accompanying scripture is from Deuteronomy 33:24-29a (KJV). Though its primary message was intended to honor veterans and acknowledge the church's anniversary, I also had in mind, my children and grandchildren:

"'The word of God for the people of God.' And the congregation responds, 'Thanks be to God.' Now be honest, did you really thank God after hearing the Scripture read this morning?

"On the other hand, did you think (to yourself, of course), 'What?' and then shake your head in dismay. I know that sometimes the words of Scripture are mystifying and confusing. Today's Scripture is not one I would typically have chosen, but it contains a small kernel of wisdom that I hope will become apparent later on in today's message. So be patient, please.

"According to a recent newspaper article, America is fast becoming a nation of 'nones.' Oh, I'm not talking about a woman in a religious order; I'm talking about the 19.3 percent of people in our country who check 'none' for their religious affiliation or preference. That's the highest percentage ever documented, nearly one out of five Americans.

"Then, too, there's an interesting phenomenon occurring in London that was reported by the BBC News Magazine. Here's the way it's described[1]:

> *A congregation of more than three hundred crowded into the shell of a deconsecrated church on Sunday morning.*
> *Instead of hymns, the non-faithful get to their feet to sing along to Stevie Wonder and Queen songs.*
> *There is a reading from Alice in Wonderland and a PowerPoint presentation from a particle physicist who explains the origins of antimatter theory.*
> *The audience—overwhelmingly young, white and middle class—appear excited to be part of something new and speak of the void they felt on a Sunday morning when they decided to abandon their Christian faith. Few actively identify themselves as atheists.*
> *Says one, "It's not a church; it's a congregation of unreligious people."*

"As disturbing and sobering as these trends are, they got me to think about the new generation of individuals coming up today. I wonder about the kind of legacy we, as members and friends of this congregation, ought to consider as our gift to them. There are several things that I'd like for all my children and grandchildren to possess after I'm gone. I hope this church would also claim ownership of them, so the generations to come in this community could also receive these spiritual benefits. They're contained and consecrated in five texts from the Bible.

"The first is in Exodus 20 and is, of course, the Ten Commandments. Now, I choose this chapter not because I'm a legalist and not because I want my children and grandchildren to be legalists. I selected it because we just cannot find our way through life without a set of guidelines, and the Ten Commandments are among the most significant collection of such guidelines that have ever been laid down. Though framed as laws, they're mostly a set of moral principles, and they can be stated as such. The first and second—'You shall have no other gods nor bow down to them or serve them'—work by the same standard and thus form the underlying assumption of all true religion that the universe obeys a single Creator.

The third—'You shall not take the name of the Lord your God in vain'—reminds us that God's name is not to be used casually, but with honor and respect, in prayer and praise. God's mission for the world is linked to the use of the divine name. The fourth—'Remember the sabbath day, to keep it holy'—emphasizes that this day of rest is a sacred gift from God, not a burden. It leaves room for worship as a way of developing that commitment and forbids the exploitation of working people. Despite the position they hold or the kind of work they do, it reminds us that all individuals have the same human rights. The fifth—'Honor your father and your mother'—is that age, and by extension, the duly formed authority that is responsible is to be held in honor. The sixth, seventh, eighth and ninth is that no one has the right to violate another person's life, family, property or reputation. And the tenth is that the desire to possess things and people is at the root of most of the evil and suffering in the world.

"When I was in the Navy, we followed a set of principles of conduct. They were officially called the 'Uniform Code of Military Justice,' but unofficially they were known as the 'Rocks and Shoals.' They pointed out the dangers to navigation, so to speak, on which a sailor might be shipwrecked if he or she wasn't careful. The Ten Commandments are a set of principles like that—a chart of rocks and sandbars on which life can be wrecked—and on which many a life has been ruined. I want present and future generations to be able to take such a chart along with them on their voyage through life.

"The second text is from Psalm 23. I want my children and grandchildren and the people who come after us in this place to know that Psalm by heart. It pictures God not as a framer of principles but as One who cares, who feeds his flock like a shepherd, who guides them in darkness and protects them in danger, whose intention it is that they find true happiness and crowns them with goodness and mercy and long life. If the Ten Commandments remind us that there's a power and a purpose beyond the universe, then Psalm 23 tells us that that power and purpose reside in a personal God, One who has the heart to love all God's children.

"Now, these two texts, the Ten Commandments and Psalm 23, are from the Old Testament. From the New Testament, I would like to leave two others. The first is the Lord's Prayer. I don't know when I first learned this prayer. I'm sure I must have learned it from my mother, and it must have been after I shortly learned to talk. All I know is that the words of this prayer are etched so deeply in my mind that even after I've forgotten everything else I've learned, the words from the Lord's Prayer will still be there.

"I've stood at the bedside of too many who were dying to be in any doubt of this. Time after time, long after all the other responses had ceased, I have begun to pray aloud the Lord's Prayer only to see a movement of eyelids or lips of the one starting his or her walk through the Valley of the Shadow. Moreover, I have sensed the peace that came from that person as in the depths of that mind, waiting now to be set free, the words of the Lord's Prayer found their way home.

"I mentioned this to a doctor friend once. He said, 'I'm sure it's true.' Then he added, 'You know, Jim, sometimes when I have a patient in the hospital that has trouble falling asleep at night, and I'd rather not prescribe medication, I suggest that he or she just try closing their eyes and seeing how often they can recite the Lord's Prayer to themselves. More often than not, they'll drift right off before the third or fourth repetition.'

"Now, that's not because the Lord's Prayer was designed to be used as a kind of chant or mantra. It's because the Lord's Prayer goes straight to the heart of our faith. Those words that Jesus taught his disciples to pray daily amount to an acknowledgment of our right relationship with God as our Creator, Redeemer, and Sustainer. They're also the means by which we are lifted above the level where most of our lives are lived and brought into God's presence where there is peace.

"If the first New Testament text I want to leave future generations is the Lord's Prayer, the second is a single line from Matthew 25. Jesus, seated on the throne of his glory, says to those whom he is welcoming into the kingdom (and I'll read from the KJV): 'Verily I say unto you, Inasmuch as ye have done it unto one of the least of these my brethren, ye have done it unto me.' That text refers to acts of human kindness and puts in brief what is the essential requirement of our faith at its highest and best—that is to say, the essential element of life at its highest and best—that it should express itself in deeds of love.

"When I was growing up in a Federal Housing Project in San Diego during World War II, a frequent sight on the streets was an old, dilapidated truck, driven by an elderly man. Now, that's not so unusual by itself, but what was unusual were three words painted on each of the truck's panels. The words read INASMUCH GOSPEL MISSION. That name delighted me as a child. I thought it was the silliest name I'd ever heard— primarily since the old man who drove the truck was what in those days we called a 'junk' man, someone who collected bottles, papers, castoff clothing, broken furniture—anything that people didn't want any longer.

"My mother must have heard us making fun of the old man and his truck with the strange words on it because I can still remember her telling me what they meant. 'That old man,' she said, 'sells the things people give him and uses the money to help the poor. He has those words on his truck because Jesus said them. There isn't anything funny about the name Inasmuch Gospel Mission. It's a beautiful name.' Well, I want future generations to remember that text as they go through life because I want them to be happy, and the secret of making a happy life is to live for the sake of others.

"The last text I want to leave my children and grandchildren and those that come after us in this place is from the Old Testament again. It's what was read as our Scripture lesson this morning. It's part of Moses' farewell to the children of Israel before he left them for the last time, and although it was initially meant for the Hebrews, it applies to every individual. Here are Moses' words, which he hoped his hearers would always carry in their hearts. 'The eternal God,' he said, 'is your dwelling place, and underneath are the everlasting arms.' Again, I want present and future generations to remember that text because I know that times will come in their lives when it will seem that the bottom has dropped out of existence, and those words may be the only firm ground on which they can stand.

"You may recall that one episode in *The Pilgrim's Progress* has to do with this. It's in the part of the story where Christian and his companion Hopeful try to cross the river that lies between them and the beautiful city of Zion, and while wading into the water Christian loses his footing and begins to sink. Here's the scene in John Bunyan's words in Part One, Stage X:

They then addressed themselves to the water; and entering, Christian began to sink, and crying out to his good friend Hopeful, he said, 'I sink in deep waters; the billows go over

41

> *my head, all his waves go over me!' Then said the other, 'Be*
> *of good cheer, my brother, I feel the bottom, and it is good.'*

"The man who wrote those lines had to have experienced two things. He had to know what it was to have the bottom drop out of life. He also had to have discovered that underneath there are the everlasting arms of God.

"Those, then, are my endowment: the Ten Commandments, the Lord's Prayer, Psalm 23, the saying of Jesus that begins with the word 'Inasmuch' and the promise of the everlasting arms of God. They're the best gifts I could leave for my children and grandchildren. I would hope that this congregation could leave behind a similar legacy. What will those that follow us say of us? Will we be found faithful? I pray we will. Amen."

Leaning on the Everlasting Arms
What a fellowship, what a joy divine,
leaning on the everlasting arms;
what a blessedness, what a peace is mine,
leaning on the everlasting arms;
Leaning, leaning, safe and secure from all alarms;
Leaning, leaning, leaning on the everlasting arms.
WORDS: Elisha A. Hoffman, 1887 (Dt. 33:27)

❧ 13 ❧

Hearing Aids

THREE RETIREES, EACH WITH A HEARING loss, were taking a walk one beautiful March day.

One remarked to the other, "Windy, ain't it?"

"No," the second man replied, "It's Thursday."

And the third man chimed in, "So am I. Let's have a Coke."

An old joke, yes. However, to millions of people, in our country alone, it's one that is not so humorous. As Martha and I have gotten older, when traveling by automobile whose road noise complicates the hearing process, we sometimes have to laugh at ourselves when one of us completely misunderstands what the other has said. At other times, when competing with the television or outdoor yard work noises, we become irritated when asked to repeat what we said.

I have inherited some hearing loss genes. My grandparents both experienced hearing problems. My father had hearing loss and wore hearing aids. My younger brother has had to rely on hearing aids for some time. I thought that somehow I would be exempt from this problem. I would ask my wife to repeat what she said, and her usual response was, "You need to get your hearing checked."

My usual reply was, "Well, speak up and stop mumbling!"

A few years ago, I finally made an appointment to have my hearing checked. After the examination, the doctor's comment was, "You have excellent hearing… for a person your age." Gee, thanks. Talk about left-handed compliments. My problem, though, according to the audiologist, is that I cannot hear sounds in the high range frequencies. Well, I can live with that, and I did... for another couple of years.

Then, in the spring of 2013, I responded to a free seminar (lunch included) sponsored by Good Sound Audiology. It was very informative and told of a study by Johns Hopkins University School of Medicine. It found those with mild, moderate, or severe hearing loss had two to five times the risk of developing dementia over time. Since several relatives on my mother's side of the family have suffered from Alzheimer's, this caught my attention. The deciding factor for me, though, was the fact that hearing aids can stimulate the nerves to the Central Auditory System and brain, thus preventing further hearing loss. Okay, it's time to get hearing aids.

Hearing aids can be expensive... or not. It depends on what company and outlet you choose. I decided to purchase a pair manufactured by a higher-end hearing appliance. Included in the total package is a lifetime warranty on the devices, free maintenance, periodic appointments with the audiologist, and an apparatus when connected to the television, streams the sound directly to the hearing aids resulting in a more precise, sharper sound.

Though my hearing has improved in some ways, I still have problems hearing local TV newspersons. They routinely speak fast (this must be part of their training) and often slur their words in the process. Moreover, for some programs, I prefer to turn on the "closed captioning" or "subtitles" device on our television. This feature is particularly useful for watching programs imported from England. My hearing devices are programmable so that in crowded rooms or movie theaters I can turn them off quickly.

Overall, I'm happy with my hearing aids. Now when I ask my wife what she said, and before she angrily responds, I reply, "I'm sorry, I don't have my hearing aids in!" Moreover, when she mumbles a question to me (I discovered that she does do this), I come up with this retort, "I have my hearing aids on. Please enunciate... Thank you!"

He Never Said a Mumbalin' Word

They crucified my Lord, and he never said a mumbalin' word;
they crucified my Lord, and he never said a mumbalin' word;
not a word (not a word), not a word (not a word),
not a word (not a mumbalin' word).

WORDS: Afro-American spiritual

14

The Favor

WHILE AN ORDAINED MINISTER, more than fifty years now, I have asked and received favors from hundreds of people. Most of these favors have to do with forms of ministry. The pastor of a church in the United Methodist system of ministry, which we term as connectional, serves as chairperson of the church's nominating committee. I've been out of the loop about the current terminology, but it used to be called the Nominating Committee. Nevertheless, I would ask persons to serve in different capacities of leadership within the local church. Often I would characterize the request as "God could use your gifts and graces through your service and witness in this way." I am not manipulative, but rather seeing a need and filling it, in most cases, with the right persons. I always respected the one who declined the invitation and usually understood their reasons. However, when the response was "yes," my heart would fill with a sense of joy. The one accepting the offer of a ministry was not only doing me a favor but God as well.

There are other examples of persons doing me a favor. A music director who considered it an honor to select the hymns for each worship service; individuals who chose to become a participant in a Bible study group I was leading; and those who made a commitment to become a part of a Hunger Walk or who worked on a Habitat for Humanity house construction project. Those in the congregation who responded to the church's annual stewardship drive; or individuals electing to take the fifty-hour training to be consecrated as a Stephen Minister. The list of those in the church who take discipleship seriously as Christ-followers is endless, but the effect on my life is the same, though—I am grateful and encouraged. Through their dedication and commitment, they have done me a kindness.

I have been on the giving end as well. God has blessed me, countless times, that I might be a blessing to others. This attitude is typical of many who have an overwhelming sense of gratitude to God for the gift of life as well as abundant living that is meaningful as revealed through Jesus the Christ. The desire to make the words of our Lord our own grows:

> *"So I say to you, Ask, and it will be given you; search, and you will find; knock, and the door will be opened for you. For everyone who asks receives, and everyone who searches finds, and for everyone who knocks the door will be opened."* (Luke 11:9-10.)

Thus, through God's Holy Spirit, I have been privileged to be the receptacle and dispenser, the giver of many favors or blessings. This privilege, for me, is one of the great joys of being in ministry—a benefit available and open to all followers of the Way.

I fully retired (mostly) from pastoral responsibilities and duties in the local church in August 2009. Since that time, I have discovered another avenue of service as a volunteer with Neighbors Who Care, a community helping agency in Sun Lakes and south Chandler. I have described my involvement with NWC in my published memoir. All the above is a rather lengthy preface as I now describe one such experience and the reason for this particular story.

One of the requests from NWC involved providing transportation for a woman's doctor appointment. Volunteers call the day before to assure the client that a ride has been arranged and to establish a time for the pickup. All went well when I arrived at the woman's home, and she was able to see her doctor at the appointed time. I brought a book with me to read while waiting. After approximately one hour, the woman finished her appointment and was ready to go home. We had a pleasant conversation in the car, and in the process, she revealed that she was a recent widow. Her husband had died a couple of months previously. When we arrived at her house, she turned to me and said, "I wonder if you would do me a favor?"

I replied, "Sure, if I can."

Her response was, "I want to spread my husband's ashes in three different locations as per his instructions. We have a summer place in our home state, a favorite lake where he liked to fish, and the place where he grew up in another state. The problem is, the mortuary just delivered his ashes in three plastic bags but they're all crammed together in one container. I can't seem to get them out. I need your help."

I've never had such an unusual request in all my years of ministry. "Let's see what I can do," I said.

She unlocked the front door, and we went inside her home. The container for her husband's ashes (the mortuary calls them "cremains") was sitting on the dining room table. I tried to remove the plastic bag on top. Ugh, it wouldn't move. I tried a few more times, but it was useless.

"I'm afraid the only way to remove the top bag so that all the others can be removed, is to put a hole in it and drain the contents into a bowl. Would you feel alright if I did that? I asked.

"If it has to be done, please do it," she said firmly.

I did. In the process, the dust from the ashes of the husband's cremains got all over my hands and arms (I was a wearing a short-sleeve shirt, fortunately), as well as her kitchen countertop. The woman didn't seem bothered that part of her husband was going down the drain. However, after the first bag was removed, the others were quickly removed without further extraction of ashes.

I washed the dust off my hands and arms, and the woman expressed her thanks. It was an odd experience, but she viewed it as a favor!

Lord, I Want to Be a Christian (vs. 2)
Lord, I want to be more loving in my heart;
Lord, I want to be more loving in my heart (in my heart).
In my heart, (in my heart),
In my heart, (in my heart),
Lord, I want to be more loving in my heart (in my heart).
WORDS: Afro-American spiritual

15

Veterans Day

VETERANS DAY IS AN OFFICIAL United States holiday that honors those who have served in the U.S. Armed Forces, also known as veterans. A federal holiday, it is observed on November 11. It coincides with other holidays such as Armistice Day and Remembrance Day, days that are celebrated in other parts of the world marking the anniversary of the end of World War I. Major hostilities of World War I were formally ended at the 11th hour of the 11th day of the 11th month of 1918, when the Armistice with Germany went into effect. An armistice is a peace agreement.

U.S. President Woodrow Wilson first proclaimed Armistice Day for November 11, 1919. In declaring the holiday, he said[2]:

> *"To us in America, the reflections of Armistice Day will be filled with solemn pride in the heroism of those who died in the country's service and with gratitude for the victory, both because of the thing from which it has freed us and because of the opportunity it has given America to show her sympathy with peace and justice in the councils of the nations."*

A Congressional Act, later approved on May 13, 1938, made the 11th of November in each year a legal holiday and changed the name to Veterans Day. Most sources spell Veterans as a simple plural without a possessive apostrophe (Veteran's or Veterans').

Why am I writing about Veterans Day? It's not because Veterans Day and I have the same birth year. Nor is it because I'm a veteran. No, I'm writing about this national holiday because for a long time it was ignored, even denigrated, by some in our country.

By June 1945, Germany capitulated to Allied Forces and the following August, after the U.S. dropped atomic bombs on two of cities; Japan surrendered. Thus, hostilities ceased, and the Second World War ended. Though the U.S. population rejoiced and celebrated the coming of peace, it would be short-lived.

A mere five years later, our nation entered into a conflict between North Korea (supported by the People's Republic of China and the Soviet Union) and South Korea (backed by the United Nations). The active engagement of war would conclude three years later with the Korean peninsula being divided along the 38th Parallel and created the Korean Demilitarized Zone (DMZ), a two-mile-wide fortified buffer zone between the two Korean nations. We still have troops patrolling and guarding this area today as this conflict has not officially ended.

The U.S. government's involvement in Vietnam began as early as December 1956, escalated and intensified until our soldiers withdrew in April 1975—more than eighteen years! This war was a very unconventional and unpopular one in the eyes of many citizens of our country. The movement against this involvement began with demonstrations in 1964 and grew in strength in later years. The polarization between those who advocated continued participation and those who wanted peace accelerated.

The American people were sick and tired of war. Television networks showed the brutality and ugliness of war on nightly newscasts. Many of our young people, drafted into military service, were being killed, maimed, or severely traumatized emotionally. Antiwar protesters aimed their unrest and distaste toward returning soldiers, sailors, marines, and aviators. Never before in our history had military personnel been treated so poorly. Honestly, it was a sense of shame.

This disrespectful attitude lasted for quite a while. A general feeling of mistrust toward our government and military leadership continued until the events of September 11, 2001. After the shock of these terrorist attacks, the U.S. went on the offensive, and a new wave of patriotism swept across our land. Those involved in the military were lionized and respected, and feelings of gratitude for those who had previously served our nation emerged. The wounds had commenced healing.

I occasionally wear a ball cap that proclaims my two-week cruise on the U.S.S. Ticonderoga, a naval aircraft carrier that has since been mothballed. I've had strangers come up to me and say, "Thanks for your service." This appreciation has only occurred in recent years. Restaurants will serve free meals to veterans on Veterans Day. Our church, for the past several years, has offered a "Tribute to Veterans" choral program in which three high school choirs participate with our church choir. When it comes time to sing the Armed Forces Service songs, veterans who served in the various branches stand as "their song" is sung. It's an emotional time; the high school youth are thrilled and awed, and it's about time. I'll end this chapter by sharing a poem that I've used many times in honoring veterans in worship. It is written by Anthony Barton Hinkle, a retired editorial columnist for the Richmond Times-Dispatch newspaper. It is entitled, "What Is a Veteran?":

> *Some veterans bear visible signs of their service: a missing limb, a jagged scar, a certain look in the eye.*
> *Others may carry the evidence inside them: a pin holding a bone together, a piece of shrapnel in the leg—or perhaps another sort of inner steel: the soul's ally forged in the refinery of adversity.*
> *Except in parades, however, the men and women who have kept America safe wear no badge or emblem.*
> *You can't tell a vet just by looking.*
> *He is the cop on the beat who spent six months in Saudi Arabia sweating two gallons a day making sure the armored personnel carriers didn't run out of fuel.*
> *He is the barroom loudmouth, dumber than five wooden planks, whose overgrown frat-boy behavior is outweighed a hundred times in the cosmic scales by four hours of exquisite bravery near the 38th parallel.*
> *She—or he—is the nurse who fought against futility and went to sleep sobbing every night for two solid years in Da Nang.*
> *He is the POW, who went away one person and came back another—or didn't come back AT ALL.*

He is the Quantico drill instructor who has never seen combat—but has saved countless lives by turning slouchy, no-account rednecks and gang members into Marines, and teaching them to watch each other's backs.

He is the parade-riding Legionnaire who pins on his ribbons and medals with a prosthetic hand.

He is the career quartermaster who watches the ribbons and medals pass him by.

He is the three anonymous heroes in The Tomb of the Unknowns, whose presence at the Arlington National Cemetery must forever preserve the memory of all the anonymous heroes whose valor dies unrecognized with them on the battlefield or in the ocean's sunless deep.

He is the old guy bagging groceries at the supermarket— palsied now and aggravatingly slow—who helped liberate a Nazi death camp and who wishes all day long that his wife were still alive to hold him when the nightmares come.

He is an ordinary and yet an extraordinary human being—a person who offered some of his life's most vital years in the service of his country, and who sacrificed his ambitions so others would not have to sacrifice theirs.

He is a soldier and a savior and a sword against the darkness, and he is nothing more than the finest, greatest testimony on behalf of the finest, greatest nation ever known.

So remember, each time you see someone who has served our country, just lean over and say Thank You. That's all most people need, and in most cases it will mean more than any medals they could have been awarded or were awarded.

Two little words that mean a lot, "THANK YOU."

"It is the soldier, not the reporter, who has given us freedom of the press. It is the soldier, not the poet, who has given us freedom of speech. It is the soldier, not the campus organizer, who has given us the freedom to demonstrate. It is the soldier, who salutes the flag, who serves beneath the flag, and whose coffin is draped by the flag, who allows the protestor to burn the flag."

The closing hymn for this chapter, "Onward, Christian Soldiers," was considered "too war-like" by some pastors and congregations, and was dropped from some hymnals. With concepts reminiscent to The Crusades, 1095-1291, some thought the words of this hymn offensive to non-Christians.

However, look at the words. Are not the followers of Christ still at war "against the evils we deplore"? Aimlessness and apathy; the spiritually empty; abuse, addictions, and harassment of all kinds; world hunger; environmental concerns; bigotry and prejudice; fighting for the marginalized and disenfranchised, the homeless, the poor, and families with low-incomes; the least, the lost, and the lonely just to name a few.

Onward, Christian Soldiers

Onward, Christian soldiers, marching as to war,
with the cross of Jesus going on before.
Christ, the royal Master, leads against the foe;
forward into battle see his banners go!
Onward, Christian soldiers, marching as to war,
with the cross of Jesus going on before.

WORDS: Sabine Baring-Gould, 1864 (2 Tim. 2:3)

16

Author

THERE'S ANOTHER AUTHOR in our family—my wife, Martha. She compiled several stories that she had previously written as assignments for various writer's groups of which she was a participant. Though she witnessed some of the difficulties I had in getting my memoir in print, she courageously moved ahead, contracting with a different publisher (I'm using that one for this book) and seeing her project to completion in the early months of 2014.

Martha describes her book, *Out of My Mind*, as an eclectic collection of engaging narratives, developed as her mind was set free to play. It is that... and more.

When asked about the title of Martha's book, I have explained it this way: "After more than fifty-five years of marriage, Martha has wondered, 'I must have been out of my mind!'" There are some things I cannot resist saying.

My wife has been a life-long singer, a talented soprano who often is asked to sing solos at memorial services, weddings, church services, and community programs. Though music feeds her soul, she asserts that writing feeds her spirit. She had, for a long time, encouraged me to write the stories of my life. After I had accomplished this task, she was inspired to publish her essays, fictional material, and faith-inspired non-fiction. She had included some speeches given when she was part of the National Association of Insurance Women (NAIW), competing and winning on regional and national levels.

Some of her narrations are funny, some are sad, but most center on the everyday difficulties of modern life. All are remarkable creations to her as expressions of something deep inside responding wonderfully as her mind drifted and wandered.

There is no doubt that Martha is the better writer. I am not trying to butter her up with a compliment here. It is accurate and evident that her writing has greater depth and character when comparing the two pieces of literature. Perhaps this is because I'm writing about my life, and she includes more and broader subject matter.

Martha's publishing experience went a lot smoother than mine. She researched several publishers before finally deciding on a specific one. It was a beneficial choice. The costs of self-publishing were about the same, but her process was less complicated and frustrating. Before submitting her material to the publisher, she made use of a line-editing program called "Grammarly" that was available to download on the Internet. This program facilitated the time involved in proofreading immensely.

Conversely, I had three friends helping me with the proofreading phase. However, my publisher's people responsible for this task would fail to make the corrections or would assign someone new to the project and fail to bring a new person up to date. Also, I discovered my publisher used the standard Spell Check program in Microsoft's Word. I had written about a pig-like desert animal from the peccary family in Arizona called a *javelina*. The spelling and grammar feature from Word changed it to "javelin," meaning a spear. Presently, as I have just typed the word "javelina" above, Word automatically underlines it in red and wants me to correct the misspelling. Yes, Martha made the right choice for a publisher.

Both of us wrote to express portions of our lives so that our children and grandchildren would have something tangible in remembering us. I'm not so sure this has or will happen. The printed page is fast becoming out of style as more and more persons, especially the younger ones, are turning to their electronic devices for quicker information. Martha's publisher, at least, made her book available in e-book form. Did I tell you that besides being beautiful, Martha is brilliant?

Let All the World in Every Corner Sing

Let all the world in every corner sing: my God and King!
The heavens are not too high, God's praise may thither fly;
the earth is not too low, God's praises there may grow.
Let all the world in every corner sing: my God and King!

WORDS: George Herbert, 1633

17

Twenty-Fifth Anniversary

IN MY MEMOIR, *This Is My Story, This Is My Song*, I wrote about my experience of starting a new congregation. The observant reader will note that very few pages were devoted to this time in my life. Gold Canyon UMC had its first worship service in the cafetorium (combination of cafeteria and auditorium) of an elementary school in January 1989. Though the first year with this young church was exciting, it was also exhausting. In all honesty, I have to say that the highlight of my three years with this congregation was the birth of our second granddaughter.

I don't want to repeat the struggles I had with some of the conference leadership and a handful (yes, they were) of the church members. Suffice it to say that I was glad, after three years, to be appointed to another church.

In all fairness, the pastor who followed me did a marvelous job. If my memory serves me, he must have stayed with the Gold Canyon church for a total of six years. During that time, the congregation was able to purchase some land (not sure of the total acreage, but it was substantial). The property was located on the main street with excellent visibility and curb appeal. In 1996, the first phase building project was constructed and completed. This project boosted the morale of the congregants, and the church grew to number over five hundred persons!

A few years later, another pastor was appointed to the Gold Canyon church. The growth increased to the point where another building project saw the construction of the sanctuary that would hold twelve hundred persons. Today its membership is around nine hundred, but winter visitors who live in the area push attendance during that season close to 2,500 each week!

January 2014, saw the church celebrate its twenty-fifth anniversary. Martha and I were invited to the celebration. I would participate in the two traditional Sunday morning worship services (they also have a contemporary Praise service and an afternoon Country Western worship event). The music program is tremendous with 75-100 in the adult choir. Also, a children's choir is offered, two handbell choirs, an orchestra, a Country Western group, and a Praise Band.

Gold Canyon UMC has a myriad of opportunities in Christian education, local and international missions, small groups, Bible study, women's groups, and dinner groups. It even has a class to help members handle their finances called Financial Peace University. The baby that I assisted in bringing into the world in 1989 (think midwife) has grown into a mature, responsible, active adult—a Christ-follower.

The hurt and disappointment I experienced while trying to serve as pastor of this congregation have diminished. Healing has taken place, and I'm proud, but also humbled, that I had a small part in the history of this church. I would like, however, to pass on some advice to this dynamic congregation lest they lose sight of why they exist.

There was a story that ran several years ago in the newspaper that showed a photo of a woman leaning over and listening to a man's chest. The caption under the picture read, "Woman listens to the heartbeat of her only son." The accompanying article talked about how the woman's son was killed in a tragic automobile accident. However, through the miracle of organ donation, some of his organs could be harvested and passed on to others needing transplants. In this case, she was listening to her son's heartbeat as its rhythmic beat gave life to someone else.

I wonder if God were to put his ear to this church, would he hear the heartbeat of his only Son? If God were to put his ear to our chest, would he hear the pulse of his only Son? If God were to put his ear to our children and grandchildren, would he hear the heartbeat of his only Son? Would God hear the heartbeat of his only Son, whose heart was broken so that ours might be mended? Through our faith, can others hear the rhythmic beat of God's heart—a heart that pulsates with love and grace? I pray so.

James D. Wood

We'll Understand It Better By and By

Temptations, hidden snares often take us unawares,
and our hearts are made to bleed for a thoughtless word or deed;
and we wonder why the test when we try to do our best,
but we'll understand it better by and by.
By and by, when the morning comes,
when the saints of God are gathered home,
we'll tell the story how we've overcome,
for we'll understand it better by and by.

WORDS: Charles A. Tindley, ca. 1906 (1 Cor. 13:12)

18

Itinerancy

WHEN UNITED METHODIST MINISTERS are ordained, they become part of an itinerant ministry. This system of ministry means they agree to travel from place to place, from one appointment to another, from one congregation to another. All ministers are under the authority of a bishop who, in consultation with his or her cabinet (district superintendents and others), make the appointments. Occasionally a minister will be deemed indispensable and irreplaceable to a particular church and will be reappointed to that congregation year after year after year. At least it seems so to me for I have known such pastors to serve in the same appointment for twenty, thirty, and even forty years. This notion does not appear to fit the description of itinerant ministry as defined in the *Book of Disciple of The United Methodist Church*. Enough said.

Well, maybe not enough. In a recent "Ask the UMC" article, a further explanation of this system was offered[3]:

> *Our unique system of deploying clergy has its roots in the earliest days of Methodism. John Wesley, the founder of the Methodist movement, preached up to 40,000 sermons in his lifetime. He was an "itinerant" preacher, traveling from town to town in England, setting up Methodist societies.*
> *"John Wesley believed that itinerant preachers who moved from place to place were more effective than those who settled in, grew comfortable, and wore out what they had to say," says the Rev. Belton Joyner.*

> *In a letter to the Rev. Samuel Walker in 1756, Wesley wrote, "We have found by long and consistent experience that a frequent exchange of preachers is best. This preacher has one talent, that another; no one whom I ever yet knew has all the talents which are needful for beginning, continuing, and perfecting the work of grace in a whole congregation."*
>
> *In the early days of Methodism in America, a pastor—most often a circuit rider—might be appointed to half of a state or more. His* [at that time, only males] *appointment might be for only three months, after which he moved to another circuit. Thousands of the oldest United Methodist congregations today trace their history to a circuit rider.*
>
> *This traveling from place to place to begin Methodist societies was adapted for the Methodist congregations many of these early societies would become after the establishment of the Methodist Episcopal Church in 1784. It thus became the basis of the itinerant system The United Methodist Church uses today.*
>
> *United Methodist pastors are sent, not called or hired. "Itinerancy" refers specifically to the commitment of pastors to go and serve wherever their bishops send them. "Appointment" is the action taken by bishops. These are different, yet related. Clergy in The United Methodist Church commit to serve where their bishop appoints them. Appointments are typically for one year at a time, though the bishop may move any itinerant pastor at any time. The goal of the appointment process is to match as much as possible the gifts and graces of the particular pastor or deacon with the ministry needs of a particular congregation or ministry setting. In this "serial leadership" of consecutive pastors and deacons—no two are alike—over time, the combination of skills blends to form a broad base of developed ministries.*

Whew. Even before becoming ordained as a United Methodist minister, I had traveled from place to place. First, with my parents from Nebraska (my birthplace); then to Bishop, California, for a few months.

Then my parents moved to San Diego, and we lived in a couple of different homes before my father got a job with Consolidated Aircraft during World War II. From there we moved to Pacific Beach where we lived in a Federal Housing Project; later to National City and my parent's first house as homeowners. After my high school graduation, we moved to Chula Vista. Seven different homes altogether, and there could be a couple more of which I'm completely unaware.

Martha and I got married while I still had a few months left on my U.S. Navy active duty obligation. We lived in four different homes before our decision to attend seminary in Denver, Colorado. Now the fun begins, and the meaning of itinerancy becomes more evident.

Two different homes in Long Beach, California—our first appointment. Two separate homes in Yuma, Arizona—our beginning as desert dwellers. One home in Chandler and two more in Mesa (a temporary apartment while our first home was being built). Then a rental in Gold Canyon, two more in Phoenix (the first being a home known as the district parsonage), and another in Peoria. After retirement, we lived in one in South Chandler (a rental) while our home was being built in Sun Lakes. Finally, our retirement home in Sun Lakes where we have lived since 2004. Did you keep count? Thirteen different places we called home during the time we served eight congregations following ordination. Then another eleven previously—altogether twenty-four homes in which I have lived in the eighty years of my life! Eleven rentals, seven parsonages (church-owned residences), and six homes of our own (bank mortgages, actually). Though we have lived in our Sun Lakes retirement home for the past fourteen years, much longer than anywhere else, that's still an average of a little more than three years in any one place.

When we traveled to England for the church exchange program in the summer of 2002, I visited some folks who had lived in the same home for fifty years. They had never traveled more than fifty miles away from home. How nice… and (for me) unexciting.

Oh, I almost forgot. My wife and I have talked recently about downsizing from our present home, maybe to something smaller like one of the Villas in Sun Lakes. However, after comparing the prices and considering the wear and tear of moving we have pretty much decided against this plan for the future. There is one last move we will be forced to make—our niche in The Gardens of the Sun Lakes United Methodist Church. It will be a little cramped, but the view of the fountain across from us is fabulous!

Where He Leads Me

I can hear my Savior calling, I can hear my Savior calling,
I can hear my Savior calling,
"Take thy cross and follow, follow me."
Where he leads me I will follow, where he leads me I will follow,
where he leads me I will follow;
I'll go with him, with him all the way.

WORDS: E. W. Blandy, 1890 (Mk. 8:34; Mt. 8:19)

19

Arizona Living

WE HAVE LIVED IN THE STATE of Arizona since the summer of 1974—more than forty-four years. As persons growing up in the temperate climate of southern California, we would never have guessed that we would end up spending more than half of our lives in The Grand Canyon State. We live in the Sonoran Desert where it gets sweltering heat for five months each year. Nevertheless, we have grown to love our adopted state. I developed a slide presentation that was given to the congregation at Central Hall Methodist Church in Longton, England, in the spring of 2007. It follows:

"Misconceptions about Arizona abound, mostly from people who have never visited the 48th state. Many consider Arizona to be nothing but an arid, waterless desert, cactus everywhere, full of rattlesnakes and other poisonous reptiles, dangerous spiders and scorpions all populated by cowboys and Indians. All true, but the fact is Arizona is much, much more.

"Arizona, situated in the southwest area of the United States, is bounded by California to the west, Nevada to the northwest, Utah to the north, Colorado to the northeast, New Mexico to the east, and the country of Mexico to the south. Arizona is the fifteenth largest state with an approximate population of 6.75 million inhabitants, and it is the sixth youngest in age (34.5 years). Its name comes from the Indian word *Alehzone* meaning "small spring." Originally a territory, it became the 48th state on February 14, 1912. At one time Arizona used to be known for its five major industries, all beginning with the letter "c." They are cotton, cattle, citrus, copper, and climate. However, some of these, namely cotton and citrus, have declined dramatically in the last several years.

"Arizona has two geographical, significant regions: the northern section called the Colorado Plateau, and the southern part known as the Sonoran Desert. The Mogollon Rim appears to separate, geographically, the north area from the south portion and can be cold, wet, and green. This area has lush forests and plenty of snow in the winter. Wildlife includes Bobcats, raccoons, many different species of birds including Northern Cardinals and Bald Eagles, mule deer, elk, mountain lions, and bears (Oh, my).

"The world-renowned Grand Canyon is in this region and is entirely contained within the state of Arizona. The San Francisco Peaks, located seven miles north of Flagstaff, are a volcanic mountain range. Humphreys Peak, in this range, is the highest peak in Arizona at 12,633 feet. Little known, even to most Arizonans, is a small volcanic peak north of Humphreys Peak called S P Crater. It was named by C. J. Babbitt, one of four brothers who settled in northern Arizona in the 1880s. He thought this volcanic crater looked very similar to a chamber pot. You guessed it, the "P" is for Pot, and the "S" is for, let's say, an indelicate word for human waste.

"The Colorado River, flowing at the bottom of the Grand Canyon, provides many opportunities for whitewater rafting. The Land of the Dinétah (Navajo) is in the northeast corner of the state. Monument Valley, Montezuma's Castle (ancient cliff dwellings), Canyon de Chelly, the Sedona Red Rock country, Meteor Crater, rodeos and Indian Pow-Wows, and winter sports typify the many scenic views, recreational areas, and tourist events in the Colorado Plateau.

"The Sonoran Desert is a region where we have lived during our time in Arizona. It is the most populated with the major cities of Phoenix and Tucson within its boundaries. On its western border is the Colorado River (its length is 1,450 miles) which flows south eventually emptying into the Gulf of California near the community of Yuma (our first ministerial appointment in Arizona). This area features the King of Arizona mountain range and contains a myriad of wildlife including the Desert bighorn sheep. Other "critters" making their home in the Sonoran Desert include coyotes, Gila monsters, javelinas, owls, horned toads, tortoises, rabbits, quail, Roadrunners, hawks, vultures, and lizards.

"A joke: 'Did you know that people who move to the southern desert of Arizona have a difficult time sleeping at night?'

'No, I didn't. Why is that?'

'They have trouble sleeping because of the Snorin' Desert.'

"The most beautiful time of year in this region is springtime when the desert wildflowers and cacti are in bloom. Glorious in color are the Mexican gold poppies, blooming aloe vera, and the Saguaro and Ocotillo cacti. Tourists from out-of-state and visitors from other countries are usually captivated by our beautiful sunsets. Also, Ostrich farms where one can enjoy a taste of "the other red meat," are an attraction. The London Bridge (transported stone by stone from England) spans the Colorado River in Lake Havasu City. The sand dunes outside Yuma, hot air balloon rides during the winter months, and the historic town of Tombstone are among tourist attractions. Tombstone, especially, populated with 'sunshine girls' and shady characters, and where the famous Gunfight at the O.K. Corral took place on October 26, 1881, is a delightful visit.

"Besides the town of Tombstone, Arizona has many other unusual sounding names for its communities. There is Mexican Water, Tortilla Flat, Grasshopper, Happy Jack, Turkey Flat, Punkin Center, Why, Christmas, Gunsight, Strawberry, Bumble Bee, Cowlic, Wolf Hole, Wild Cow Springs, Bagdad, Valentine, Skull Valley, and Two Guns to name several.

"*Arizona ha sido influido por México, su vecino del sur, en su idioma, su cultura, la comida, la póblacion, la música, también.* Translation: 'Arizona has been influenced by Mexico, its neighbor to the south, in its language, culture, food, population, and music.' I admit one of my nieces did the translation as my own proficiency in the tongue is a bit rusty.

"Towns with Spanish names include Agua Prieta, Nogales, Ajo, San Luis, Mesa (Arizona's third largest city), Rillito, Sierra Vista, Sonoita, Palominas, Casa Grande, Santa Rosa, San Miguel, San Pedro, and La Palma. There are many others as well.

"More than one-third of Arizona's citizens are Hispanic/Latino. The illegal alien population makes up at least forty-six percent of the state's total foreign-born population and six percent of the state's total population. Unfortunately, given Arizona's proximity to Mexico, an average of 1,374 aliens are apprehended at Arizona's border sector each day. In 2013, there were more than two hundred deaths as persons died from thirst and the desert heat in their attempt to find employment and a better way of life in Arizona.

"Nevertheless, the Hispanic and Latino culture that Arizona shares with our amigos from the south are very evident and both diverse and fascinating. Besides merchants selling everything from traditional pottery, clothes, and jewelry; many restaurants and cafes offer some of the best in real authentic Mexican food. Yum! Moreover, there are often Mexican fiestas with dancing and music that are fun to experience.

"Arizona has three state-owned universities. The University of Arizona in Tucson, with 40,000 plus students; Northern Arizona University in Flagstaff, with more than 25,000 students; and Arizona State University in Tempe, with close to 75,000 students, making it the largest university in the United States.

"The capital of Arizona is in Phoenix. Incorporated February 25, 1881, the Navajos called it Hoozdo or 'the place is hot.' The Apaches called Phoenix by the name Fiinigis (you may have to use your imagination here). Phoenix is the largest capital city in the United States with a population of 1.6 million persons. It is the fifth largest city in the country, recently surpassing Philadelphia. Only New York City, Los Angeles, Chicago, and Houston have more people than Phoenix. Arizona's capital is called "The Valley of the Sun," appropriate enough as it has 320 sunny days per year with an average rainfall being about 8 inches. Half of this figure comes to the area in the form of "monsoon" summer rain. Violent dust storms, called "haboobs," can and do occur in the Phoenix area.

"Phoenix is home to several professional sports teams. It has the Arizona Cardinals (football), the Phoenix Suns (men's basketball), the Phoenix Mercury (women's basketball), the Phoenix Coyotes (hockey), the Arizona Rattlers (Arena Football), Phoenix Rising (soccer), and the Arizona Diamondbacks (baseball). Arizona also plays host to many major league baseball teams who play in the Cactus League during spring training.

"Arizona is a favorite for many folks who live out-of-state during the winter months. These retirees are known affectionately as 'snowbirds.' They come to our state by the hundreds of thousands each year to enjoy the warm weather, golf, swimming in January, tennis, pickleball, hiking, and a myriad of other activities that the area offers."

There you have it… A somewhat comprehensive tour of the state that we have come to love. The decision to make Arizona our permanent home was made sometime around 1985. At that time, the Desert Southwest Conference of United Methodism (Arizona and southern Nevada) was created. It separated from the existing Pacific Southwest Conference (then consisting of Arizona, southern Nevada, southern California, Hawaii, and one church on the island of Guam). Pastors were given the opportunity to stay in Arizona or request a transfer to the parent Conference. We chose to stay in Arizona.

Do we like everything about Arizona? No. The heat every summer can get oppressive. Each year, as we approach the summer months, a favorite newspaper columnist promotes a limerick contest. Contestants are encouraged to write about Phoenix's hot weather with the top winners given tickets to Diamondback games. Here are some of the entries:

> *Ninety degrees is the low.*
> *At least there's no worry of snow.*
> *One twenty's the high*
> *I'm soon gonna cry*
> *'Cause my AC's not cold and won't blow.*

Another one:

> *There was a guy new to the state*
> *Whose cleverness was his best trait.*
> *His car baked in the heat*
> *So he bought some raw meat*
> *And cooked it up there on a plate.*

Well, enough of that. You get the point.

We have problems every year with wildfires in the high country. They are usually caused by careless campers or intentionally set by arsonists. It continues to anger us the number of small children that drown in family swimming pools because their parents or other responsible adults don't oversee them. Finally, we dislike the current politics in our beloved state.

I won't go into a rant here because I've already "alienated" most of you by even mentioning my distaste of the subject. Enough said.

I want to conclude this particular chapter on a "high note" by sharing a song with words written by our church's music director, Cris Temple Evans, and her sister Lela Temple. Its tune is from "Winter Wonderland" and, though not copyrighted, permission is given to print the lyrics:

> *Phoenix Wonderland*
> *Palm trees sway, are you listenin'?*
> *In the pool, water's glistenin'.*
> *A warm sunny day, we like it that way,*
> *Livin' in a Phoenix wonderland.*
> *Gone away is the blizzard.*
> *Here to stay is the lizard.*
> *A warm sunny day, we like it that way,*
> *Livin' in a Phoenix wonderland.*
> *In the desert, we will have a picnic.*
> *Cactus, sand, and rattlesnakes and sun.*
> *Christmas dinner is a big tradition,*
> *With pinto beans and tacos by the ton.*
> *Later on, we'll perspire.*
> *Temperatures rising higher.*
> *A warm sunny day, we like it that way,*
> *Livin' in a Phoenix wonderland.*

This Is My Father's World

This is my Father's world, and to my listening ears all
nature sings, and rounds me rings the music of the spheres.
This is my Father's world: I rest me in the thought of
rocks and trees, of skies and seas; his hand the wonders wrought.

WORDS: Maltbie D. Babcock, 1901

∽ 20 ∽

A Myth Dismissed

FAMILY HISTORY CAN BE INTRIGUING, disappointing, laughable, mystifying, sad, and even provoking pride. My father, as I mentioned in my memoir, was an inveterate storyteller. He passed on to those of us in the Wood family many accounts of his life and the lives of those who preceded him—parents, cousins, grandparents, and great-grandparents. Some of the information Dad shared was an unconfirmed rumor, and he would quickly add, "So I've been told."

For the past several years, I've had an interest in family history and genealogy. I've been curious about my roots and the people whose Deoxyribonucleic acid (DNA) comprise mine. DNA is a molecule that encodes the genetic instructions used in the development and functioning of all known living organisms and many viruses. Not long ago, I submitted a sample of my DNA to AncestryDNA.com to discover something about my ethnic background, where my relatives lived. The results were somewhat, but not entirely, surprising. My ethnicity estimate shows 39 percent from Ireland, 17 percent from Scandinavia (Norway, Sweden, and Denmark), and 16 percent from Western Europe (Germany, Poland, Austria, Hungary, Switzerland, the Netherlands, Belgium, France, and northern Italy). Surprisingly, since Wood is an English name, only 12 percent from Britain. The remaining 9 percent were from the Iberian Peninsula (Spain, Portugal, and Sicily) with another 7 percent from "Trace Regions" such as Italy, Greece, Finland, and Northwest Russia. Finally, 1 percent Jewish… *Hmmm, I knew I was related to Adam and Eve.* In other words, I'm a mixed breed, a mongrel, a mutt. Wow, or should I say, "Sure and begorrah! Saints be praised," my ancestors got around!

But I digress. Whenever the topic of my relatives came up, my father would mention his grandmother, Elizabeth Jeffers Lee, who married Isaac Monroe Wood in 1875. She was twenty-two, and he was twenty-five. Both were born about a decade before the start of the Civil War, she in Missouri and he in Indiana. Isaac and Betty had six children (one died at birth), all born in Missouri. My grandfather, James Martin Wood, was their fourth child.

My father, whenever he brought up the subject of Grandma Wood, would say, "It's possible she was related to Robert E. Lee, the General of the Confederate Army." Whoa! Nevertheless, I didn't give this much thought until several years after my father's death. That's when I started looking into our family tree.

What I discovered was that my great-grandmother, Elizabeth Jeffers Lee, had a great-grandfather Richard Bland Lee (1753-1820), born in Stafford County, Virginia. General Robert E. Lee was from Virginia, and his famous home was Arlington, now our national cemetery. Robert E. Lee's father was Henry ("Light-Horse Harry") Lee and Henry's brother was Richard Bland Lee. This man was the uncle of the famous Civil War General!

In reading an e-book entitled, *Clouds of Glory: The Life and Legend of Robert E. Lee*, by Michael Korda, I ran across this interesting piece of information[4]:

> *By 1820 three philanthropic Virginians, two of them relatives of Robert E. Lee—Henry Clay, John Randolph, and Richard Bland Lee, co-founders of the American Colonization Society—had already made ambitious plans and raised money to create Liberia. The capital of Liberia was named Monrovia to honor another Virginian, President James Monroe. These men set the process in motion by sending freed blacks there.*

Ancestry.com directed me to the mentioned above Richard Bland Lee, but I noticed an apparent discrepancy—another Richard Bland Lee

(1761-1827), eight years younger than my ancestor. Both were married to women with the first name of Elizabeth (my great grandmother's first name). However, their last names were different: Collins versus Scott. It turned out, after doing further research, that Robert E. Lee's uncle, Richard Bland Lee, was married to Elizabeth Collins. My great-grandmother's Richard Bland Lee was married to Elizabeth H. Scott. These two latter ones were married (she was thirteen, and he was twenty-four) and raised twenty-one children in Kentucky. Remember, they didn't have television in those days!

It was quite a coincidence that these two men had the very same middle name. I mean, Bland is not very common and was probably a family name. The great-grandmother of Richard Lee who is related to the Confederate General was Mary Bland (1704-1764). How my relative came by his middle name, who knows? I can't say I was disappointed. Though revered by many in both the south and north following the War Between the States, as the Civil War was later referred to by those in the South, Robert E. Lee's demeanor and attitude toward black slaves were typical of many plantation owners during and following the antebellum period.

The website FamousKin.com lists the names of those related to famous people. I looked up General Robert E. Lee's name to see if my name appeared. Of course, it didn't, but I got a good laugh at the names of some on the list. Besides several presidents, these were included: Susan B. Anthony, Franklin D., and Eleanor Roosevelt, Bing Crosby, Queen Elizabeth II, Marilyn Monroe, Frank Lloyd Wright, Sandra Day O'Connor, Walt Disney, Lee Harvey Oswald, Brad Pitt, Raquel Welch, Mitt Romney, and (wait for it)… Barack Obama![5] Oh, what fun it is to discover your ancestors.

The Battle Hymn of the Republic

Mine eyes have seen the glory of the coming of the Lord;
he is trampling out the vintage
where the grapes of wrath are stored;
he hath loosed the fateful lightning of his terrible swift sword;
his truth is marching on.
Glory, glory, hallelujah! Glory, glory, hallelujah!
Glory, glory, hallelujah! His truth is marching on.

WORDS: Julia Ward Howe, 1861

71

∾ 21 ∾

Unrevealed Until Its Season

THERE IS A BEAUTIFUL SONG in our United Methodist Hymnal composed by Natalie Sleeth. At the seminary I attended, she was the wife of one of my professors. The song's title is "Hymn of Promise," and the message it conveys is hope of the resurrection following death. The refrain of this hymn contains these words: "…unrevealed until its season, something God alone can see."

How accurate is this statement. To have faith that God has something beautiful planned for us after we finish with life as we know it is to trust that God's love for us continues beyond the point of death.

Even in the midst of living, we experience God's revealing pleasant surprises that we never thought could happen or never dreamed of occurring.

I wrote about some serendipitous happenings in my young adult life when I first met and started dating the woman who would be my wife, Martha. Then, following our marriage and the birth of our two oldest children, God's calling me to ordained ministry, something God alone could see. I can recall a multitude of life experiences that occurred that was unanticipated but came as a beautiful surprise from God. "Do you have eyes, and fail to see? Do you have ears, and fail to hear?" (Mark 8:18.)

Martha's father died from a gun accident when she was almost two-years-old. Her mother, for reasons unknown to us, chose to cut herself off from her family and her husband's family.

Consequently, for thirty-six years Martha knew nothing about her family on either side. Then, in 1976, an unrevealing from God. Martha's cousin, a Presbyterian minister's wife, encouraged her to attend a family reunion in West Virginia. We went, and Martha discovered family she never knew existed. She was given photos of her father and his parents and many other relatives. Unrevealed until its season, something God alone can see.

Our oldest daughter was diagnosed with breast cancer in 1998. An aggressive type, she elected to have the full treatment that included surgery, chemotherapy, and radiation. Not a pleasant surprise from God except that this was twenty years ago, and she has since been cancer free. Unrevealed until its season, something God alone can see.

We adopted our youngest daughter while I was in my first year of seminary, and the process of adoption took less than four months. We love our daughter very much, but we were aware of a particular void in her life. Several years ago, we made an effort to find out the background material regarding her biological parents. Though the information we received was helpful and included some pertinent facts about her birth father and mother, it didn't reveal their names or locations. We were at a dead end.

In 2013, our adopted daughter and her husband started their own automotive repair business in Tempe, Arizona. Her husband would sometimes do barter work for his customers. One of these was a private investigator. He indicated that he could cut through the judicial system's red tape and get the kind of information we had earlier failed to receive.

Though both were apprehensive and somewhat nervous, they agreed to allow this customer to do an investigation. He was able to get a judge in Colorado to open the court's files and obtained the names and locations of her birth parents. Unrevealed until its season, something God alone can see.

Postscript: our daughter has been in touch with both biological parents by telephone. The father initially was receptive and excited to hear from his daughter, forty-four years later. The mother was cautious and somewhat reluctant. However, the situation has reversed. No further word from the father and the mother agreed to meet with Kathryn in Albuquerque, New Mexico. Their meeting was successful regarding getting acquainted and sharing histories. They continue to keep in touch, and the corner of emptiness that had plagued our daughter is being filled with newfound love. Something God alone can see. Thank you, Holy One.

James D. Wood

There's a Wideness in God's Mercy

There's a wideness in God's mercy like the wideness of the sea;
there's a kindness in God's justice, which is more than liberty.
For the love of God is broader than the measure of our mind;
and the heart of the Eternal is most wonderfully kind.

WORDS: Frederick W. Faber, 1854

22

Grumbles and Gripes

IN ONE OF THE NOVELS written by Jo Nesbø (pronounced *yew nesba*), the main character, a homicide cop in Oslo, Norway, by the strange and laughable name of Harry Hole, says, "I'm pushing forty and I've started to enjoy grumbling. Anything wrong with that?"

Well, I'm pushing eighty and, though I'm usually even-tempered, there are some things, petty things to be sure, which drive me crazy. I used this expression one time in a conversation with my son, and he came back with this retort: "Dad, with you that distance is not very far." Nevertheless, as I have grown older, I've developed several pet peeves. Unfortunately, the list keeps growing.

Oh, in case you're wondering, a pet peeve is a minor annoyance that an individual identifies as particularly irritating to him or herself, to a higher degree than others may find it. Its first usage was around 1919 (oddly enough toward the end of World War I). The term is back-formation from the 14th-century word peevish, meaning "ornery or ill-tempered."

With all this in mind, and trying not to sound like Andy Rooney of TVs *60 Minutes* fame, and asking your forgiveness of a sometimes grumbling old man, here's my list of pet peeves, annoying ones that are in no particular order of importance:

- People who chew with their mouths open—disgusting!
- Poor driving etiquette—discourteous and road rage drivers (you're an accident waiting to happen).

- Not washing hands after using a public restroom (makes me wonder if I should shake hands with you).
- Talking behind someone's back—does this make you feel superior?
- Texting or using the cell phone while driving (come on, Arizona, make a law).
- Loud cell phone conversations in public (you don't want me joining something that should be private).
- Adults talking on their cell phones while ignoring their children (you'll be sorry because they grow up too fast).
- Juveniles (and adults who should know better) holding fingers in a "V" behind someone's head while getting their photo taken. Hey, search the dictionary for the word "cuckold." Ignorance is bliss.
- People with their smartphones who don't look where they're walking.
- Men and adolescent boys wearing their baseball caps turned around backward—only looks cute on the little guys.
- Movies and television programs that show criminals wearing a cross or crucifix around the neck.
- People who drink and then drive—get a designated driver!
- Parking a car across two spaces.
- Children throwing temper tantrums in public.
- Teens who whine about their parents telling them what to do.
- Athletes who emulate prison thugs by getting numerous body tattoos—what fantastic role models you are!
- Overuse of filler words such as "you know," "no problem," "actually," "basically," "cool," and "perfect." Also, using the word "like" or "just" before every sentence. It is poor communication and a bad habit.
- Food servers who say, "I'll just grab you some water." Don't grab some water, just bring it to me.
- Newscast announcers who, when describing traffic conditions, refer to vehicle collisions as a "crash." We used to call them "accidents," but apparently now we prefer to describe the sound collisions make!
- People who throw trash from their car windows (usually cigarette butts) as they drive—give a hoot and don't pollute!

- People with bad breath who talk right in your face.
- Body odor—come on, you really think it's manly?
- People who don't clean up after their dogs—Sun Lakers pay attention.
- People who use the word "So" before answering a question. "So, what we want to do is this…"
- Lousy service at restaurants—and you expect a 20 percent tip?
- T-shirts and/or bumper stickers with obscene words.
- Persons with a limited vocabulary who drop the f-bomb in every sentence—your mother would be so proud!

However, the most annoying and rudest pet peeve is one that grates on my sensibility. It is the casual disregard of the commandment, "You shall not make wrongful use of the name of the LORD your God, for the LORD will not acquit anyone who misuses his name" (Exodus 20:7.)

Strange how unbelievers and even some who profess belief often profane the LORD's name and how those not a part of the Christian faith disrespect the name of our Savior. Is it an unholy habit or some unknown anger at God that creates such ugly and demeaning words? I wonder.

Turn Your Eyes upon Jesus
Turn your eyes upon Jesus,
look full in his wonderful face (wonderful face),
and the things of earth will grow strangely dim
in the light of his glory and grace.
WORDS: Helen H. Lemmel, 1922

❦ 23 ❦

Make Today Count
(a sermon)

THOUGH I ENJOY SOME grumbling, and it probably has some therapeutic benefits for the soul, that's not where I prefer to dwell. I can only sit on the pity pot for a short while. Then there comes a time to get off and get on with the business of joyful living once more. I believe this is what God intends for us, and what Jesus meant when he talked about abundant life. As I stated in the introduction to these writings, I'm a person filled to the brim with gratitude to God for the many blessings God has bestowed upon me. This joyful attitude of gratitude has instilled many beneficial characteristics in me. However, it's possible that we may miss the experience of joyful living as the difficulties and problems of everyday life seek to overwhelm us.

This overwhelming experience can happen in our spiritual life, as well. Some evangelists and preachers are so concerned about the end time, the fulfillment of prophecy and the second coming of Christ that today no longer counts much for them. They get people so worked up that they become filled with the same over concern. I've known persons so intent on the Last Judgment and the Rapture that they gave up their jobs, neglected their families and friends and missed life's daily miracles. The following words attributed to Jesus in the Gospel According to Mark are both a reminder and an invitation to us:

"But about that day or hour no one knows, neither the angels in heaven, nor the Son, but only the Father. Beware, keep alert; for you do not know when the time will come … And what I say to you I say to all: Keep awake." (Mark 13:32-33, 37.)

Any ultimate hope or vision of God's kingdom is always upheld by the meanings we find in being fully alive today. That's why we're to make each day count by being alert to its miracles and openings, its opportunities and blessings. By so doing, we'll be alert and ready for the final moment whenever it comes.

Therefore, we need this word of Jesus when we take things and people for granted and when we get our priorities confused. We need this word when we waste time by hurrying big for little reasons or trying to second-guess God. We need this word when we cloud the present moment with fear and envy or sour it with complaining self-pity and possessive demands. Jesus offers us life that is abundant and fulfilling, exciting and dynamic, and he shows us how to make today count both by lesson and example.

First, let bygones be gone. Leave behind the bitter memories that fester in us and discard the excess baggage of guilt that we so often carry around with us. Jesus encourages us to put away yesterday's regrets, the missed opportunities, the disappointed dreams, the unfulfilled intentions, the words that never got said soon enough or the wrong words spoken too soon. He invites us to lay aside the nursed grievances and resentments for hurts and betrayals that keep us separated, hostile and vengeful.

Again, there's his instruction: Don't water yesterday with tears of regret and don't blacken today with yesterday's burning resentments. Don't waste time keeping emotional ledgers and trying to even the score. Abandon the vendettas of retaliation and the silent malice of studied indifference. Forsake the entanglement of self-pity and resolve the internal strife and tension, whether directed against oneself or someone else. Jesus knew that frozen rage, self-pity, and self-condemnation make us miserable, cripple us and ruin the present moment. So He says, "Get rid of it! Don't let it diminish your stature or the excitement of living today. Come to me you who are heavy laden (with such baggage) and lay it down. Rest here with me. Live from grace. Your guilt and regret, your negative memories and suspicions are no longer necessary. Rise above them and move beyond them."

One woman who was bitterly hostile toward her sister over a disputed family discovered this. Her resentment and regret had darkened the passing years, and something crucial had almost died inside her. Then one Sunday during worship, certain words of Scripture became an invitation with her name and address on it. That afternoon she wrote a letter of love and reconciliation to her sister. She says, "When I dropped that letter in the mailbox, it was like a thousand Easter 'Alleluias!' singing inside me. The world was beautiful again, and I felt alive for the first time in years." Yes, let bygones be gone.

Second, Jesus also reminds us: Stop worrying! The interest rates on borrowed trouble are too high: nervous tension, physical fatigue, severe illness and the discontent of not feeling up to par. We also pay for worry about unstable relationships. Anxiety blocks genuine sharing with others. When we're worrisome and tense, we cannot relax and enjoy being with others and they, in turn, are not at ease with us. Chronic worriers always spread a pall of pessimism and gloom, create lonely worlds that are empty of laughter and singing, and are not pleasant to be with or around.

The most significant price we pay for worry, however, is a loss of the specialness of this present moment. If fear of tomorrow or the day after tomorrow consumes us, we'll miss the opportunities of today. One person, awakening to how run-down his life and world had become because of his worrying, conducted a study. Analyzing how he and other people worried, he concluded that 40 percent of worries are about things that never happen; 30 percent are about past decisions that we cannot change, and 12 percent are about criticism (mostly untrue) of us by others, usually arising from envy and misunderstanding. Moreover, 10 percent are about personal health which only grows worse with worry, and only 8 percent are legitimate concerns that need our attention. This analysis means that when we worry we waste a lot of time and energy. We also overlook opportunities that may never come again to us, special moments that may occur only once in our lifetime. Think of the hugs we've avoided because we were worrying, the spontaneous delights of children or grandchildren growing up, the wayside miracles in nature, the fun of playing together, the secrets that we could have known, the beauty we could have shared.

That's why Jesus reminds us of the abundant resources of faith on which we can call to reduce our anxiety and put worry behind us. He urges us to trust God with all our tomorrows, to believe God enough to face the unknown without fear. He assures us that we can rely on God's power and whatever may happen; it'll be all right, we'll make it through. With such faith awareness, we can make today count, we can share love and joy, and we can live forgiven and free. A motto that used to hang over many a household's mantles put it this way: "Fear knocked on the door. Faith answered. There was no one there." For God's sake and yours, stop worrying!

We need to remember that Jesus calls us to be open and greet life with expectation, reverence, and wonder. This approach is how Jesus lived—free from regret and worry—and his teachings ring with an invitation for us to do the same. "Look at the birds of the air," he said. "Consider the lilies of the field… Don't worry about tomorrow, for tomorrow can take care of itself… Let your light shine… Where your treasure is there will your heart be also… If your whole body is full of light, it will be radiant as a lamp shining brightly… Believe and don't be disappointed… How fortunate that you have eyes that see and ears that hear." Watch Jesus as he moves through his days with such purpose and pure enjoyment that his enemies labeled him a glutton and a drunkard. Watch him reverence God in times of prayer and meditation. Realize how he moves in rhythm with all of life in wonder and finds deeper dimensions in ordinary routines: like a woman baking bread, children at play, and guests at a wedding feast. He enters so deeply into life that everyday things take on new meaning: a sparrow, salt, weeds in the grain field, leaky wineskins, fruit on the tree at harvest, an ox's yoke, and a cup of cold water at the well. Jesus is so open and affirming in his relationships with others that he redefines the meaning of love and friendship, and of trust and commitment.

Jesus encourages us to enter life in the same way. He wants us to wonder as we wander, to touch and savor the gift of life, to receive into and reflect upon and find how uncommon the common is, to discover the extra in the ordinary.

Groups of children were once asked, "What are the twelve loveliest things you know?" These are some of their responses:

The cold of ice cream ... the scrunch of dry leaves ... the feel of clean clothes ... water running in a bath ... climbing up a hill and looking down ... the smell of a drug store ... the feeling inside when you sing ... babies smiling ... little kittens.

What would you say? Someone once wrote, "If we had a keener vision of all ordinary human life, it would be like hearing the grass grow or the squirrel's heartbeat, and we should faint from the roar which lies on the other side of silence."

When we're alert to the awakenings of the Holy Spirit in the ordinary, we'll greet each day with an eager expectancy and a sense of wonder and make every day count. Instead of borrowing trouble, life will come alive, and love will create relationships of caring and trust with God and others. Why borrow trouble when we can trust God with today and all the tomorrows that are ours? Let bygones be gone. Stop worrying. Accept our Lord's invitation to be open and greet life with expectation, reverence, and wonder. Make today count!

Wonderful Words of Life

Sing them over again to me, wonderful words of life;
let me more of their beauty see, wonderful words of life;
words of life and beauty teach me faith and duty.
Beautiful words, wonderful words, wonderful words of life.
Beautiful words, wonderful words, wonderful words of life.

WORDS: Philip P. Bliss, 1874

~ 24 ~

Hawaii Revisited

WHILE SERVING TRINITY UMC in Yuma, Arizona (1974-78), Martha and I had the opportunity to travel with a small group from the church to Hawaii. The couple organizing this event had been stationed in Hawaii while serving with the U.S. Army. They formerly belonged to one of the United Methodist churches on the island of Oahu. Through friends, they arranged for our group to attend the church's family camp in Honolulu.

The itinerary included the Polynesian Cultural Center, a Luau and Hawaiian entertainment, a trip to Pearl Harbor and a visit to the USS Arizona Memorial, and a general tour of Oahu. We were on our own for a couple of days, and we chose, along with Martha's mother and her husband who accompanied us, to visit the islands of Kauai and the big island of Hawaii. This all happened in May 1977, and the trip was beautiful and memorable.

Oh, I almost forgot to mention this. We noticed that some people emphasized the "w" in Hawaii, while others stressed the "w" as a "v" as in Havaii. I asked a man who looked to be pure Hawaiian which was correct.

He said, "We pronounce it "Havaii."

I thanked him for this information, and he replied, "You're velcome!" (Old joke, I know.)

Anyway, thirty-seven years later, I had the opportunity to revisit this paradise in the Pacific. As an aside, let me share that Martha was a participating member of the National Association of Insurance Women (NAIW). She attended a conference in Oahu a year or so later. Then, as

Regional Vice President, an area consisting of five western states including Hawaii, she was invited to attend (all expenses paid) a luncheon at the fiftieth state's annual conference.

However, in August 2014, we made the trip together. I won't go into much detail about it, though I want to mention that our plans were not "dampened" by the event of a hurricane and tropical storm—Iselle and Julio. We stayed ahead of these storms and were able to visit another of the Hawaiian Islands—Maui—staying at a condominium in the community of Lahaina. Now, for the real reason for relating this story.

I mentioned in my memoir something about the holidays I remembered as a boy growing up in Pacific Beach during the years 1942-51. In particular, I recounted memories of celebrating the May Day festivities at Bayview Terrace Elementary School, and my fifth-grade class learning a Hawaiian stick dance. I tried (apparently unsuccessfully) to pass on the words of the song we children learned.

Nevertheless, after we returned from our recent trip to Hawaii, I shared with our children that I should have asked someone who spoke Hawaiian the meaning of the words. Our son, a compulsive smartphone user, looked up the title of the song on YouTube and sent the interpretation to me. You may recall my telling that I used the words as a benediction to a memorial service for a woman who had lived in Hawaii for a large part of her life. Though I didn't translate the words (because I did not know their meaning), the woman's family was delighted!

I can now share the correct spelling with additional words and, much to my chagrin, the sense of the words—words that learned almost sixty-five years ago. Compare them with my first accounting:

O Kona Kai'Opua

O Kona kai'ōpua i ka la'I	*The cloud bank over Kona's peaceful sea*
'O pua hinano i ka mālie	*Like the hinano flower in the calm*
Holo na wai a ke kehau	*Where dusk descends with evening dew*
Ke na'u wai la nā kamali'i	*The na'u is chanted by the playful children*

Moreover, the following from the Kaleinamanu Literary Archive is an interpretation of the song's meaning[6]:

This mele (song) tells of a love affair between Liholiho (Kamehameha II) and a woman of rank. It sings of the places and activities of Kona and compares them to the deep emotions of love. They awoke in the morning, and Kamehameha saw that the sea at Keauhou was beautifully calm. Therefore, he asked the woman to go swimming. She agreed…. He told the woman to board the canoe. She said, "But I thought we'd swim here close to shore!" He answered, "No, we'll get in the canoe."…. Then Kamehameha boarded the canoe, and he began to paddle their vessel. Kamehameha was at the stern of the canoe, and the woman was at the bow. Kamehameha faced forward, and the woman faced backward. The woman wore no clothes because she had meant to go swimming. Consequently, Kamehameha could not resist the sight of her. He began to chant this mele, and then he moved to embrace her.

Probably more information than you needed, but I hope this clears up a few things. Nevertheless, it doesn't sound much like an old Hawaiian prayer suitable for closing a memorial service, does it? Well, maybe the part about being chanted by playful children… After all, I still have a lot of playful boy in me, even though, at the time of this writing, I'm a year for every trombone that led the big parade.

Near to the Heart of God

There is a place of quiet rest, near to the heart of God;
a place where sin cannot molest, near to the heart of God.
O Jesus, blest Redeemer, sent from the heart of God,
hold us who wait before thee near to the heart of God.

WORDS: Cleland B. McAfee, 1903

❧ 25 ❧

Election Day

GENERAL ELECTION DAY, November 2014, is over and done. It was not very favorable for President Barak Obama and the Democrats. It was an overwhelming landslide victory for the Republican Party, the Grand Old Party, the party of Abraham Lincoln (although he probably wouldn't recognize it if he were alive today). Most everyone over the age of fifty is aware that election tactics, both national and local, have changed for the worse. Bombarded by numerous campaign commercials on television, too many automated phone calls, and enough negative news commentary, we begin to question the very meaning of our election process.

Candidates want to appeal to our sense of duty, compassion, and patriotism. They and their outside resources, sometimes known as dark money, spend loads of dollars to play on our fears and hope to inspire us somehow along the way. In short, the election process has become mean-spirited, polarizing, divisive, and fear-inducing. This negative evolving of our election process is discouraging and distressing to me.

Tony Campolo is a former professor of sociology and leader in evangelical Christian social action, a sought-after speaker, and best-selling author of numerous books. One of his books is entitled, *Is Jesus a Republican or a Democrat?* In it he suggests this[7]:

> *The temperament of our country was liberal, and the mainline denominations created for America a God who incarnated their liberal causes.*

86

But now the pendulum has swung. Conservatism now appears to be the unstoppable social ideology. In both politics and religion (and it is often impossible to distinguish between them these days), the movement toward the right seems irresistible."

Campolo makes an important point when he says, "There is no better way for a political party to establish the legitimacy of its political point of view than to declare that Jesus is one of its members. This remaking of Jesus is not just some kind of harmless campaign technique. It is not merely something sophisticated sociological observers can pass off with a wry smile and a wave of the hand. It is not just bad religion that needs correcting. *The Bible calls it idolatry!*"[8]

I am not going to list the qualities, the good, as well as the wrong, of both political parties here. For some readers who have set their thinking in concrete, it wouldn't make any difference. Nevertheless, I do want to remind you of what it means to be a disciple of Jesus Christ in the process of electing officials to represent us locally and nationally.

I do this through an article that a colleague has written. He says, "… if we're not careful, we might begin to believe that our being opposed to this issue or that issue, and thus also being against every person who disagrees with us, is what it means to live as a follower of Jesus Christ. We might even begin to believe that the political party we support is the best embodiment of the gospel in our lives. Moreover, we would be totally wrong.

"Remember, there are Christians who support both political parties. Don't assume your party has a monopoly on God's agenda. The truth is that neither party can faithfully speak for God's mission in the world.

"Take a break from talk radio and the news on television if you find it only serves to get you all worked up about politics. Don't do things that make you mad or get you upset just for the fun of it. That only drives the entertainment industry that is news commentary. God calls us to lives graciously and generously, not bitterly.

"Pray for our leaders and candidates on both sides of the aisle and ballot. That's right, pray for them and not against them. Don't you want what is best for our country?

"Speak up and politely call for an end to negative or heated political discussion in your Sunday school class or small group. Church small groups can notoriously get lost in the weeds of politics while discussing a lesson or sharing prayer concerns. Remember, there's a fine line between sharing prayer concerns and just gossiping. Be a voice in the room that politely reminds everyone you are gathered to learn and experience God, not vent your latest political gripes.

"Go vote. Then go serve. Voting is a civic duty, and we should appreciate the freedom given to us to participate openly in the election process. But, remember, your vote is certainly not the final word on your life as a disciple of Christ. Find a way also to serve during the week of Election Day. Participate in a church activity. Give an hour to a local shelter helping those who are poor and hungry. Get out of your comfort zone and be reminded that no matter how this Election Day ends, your life as a disciple of Jesus Christ is still the most central thing as to who you are.

"Moreover, stop spreading untruths about a candidate and political parties and platforms. Refrain from name-calling. Don't believe everything you read on the Internet. Before you pass on any e-mail gossip, check out the websites of Snopes.com, Factcheck.org or Flackcheck.org for an unbiased truth or falsehood on specific subjects. Your version or someone else's slant on the truth does NOT make it accurate. Let the chain of untruth spreading end with you.

"If our churches and the people within them decide to live as the disciples we claim to be, the news in our communities might just have a story to share besides the results of the election."

At the conclusion of his chapter, Campolo summarizes with these words, "Both parties are partly right and partly wrong. I'm glad we have a two-party system in this country. And I'm glad that God belongs to neither of them." Amen, brother, amen!

'Tis So Sweet to Trust in Jesus

'Tis so sweet to trust in Jesus, and to take him at his word;
just to rest upon his promise, and to know, "Thus saith the Lord."
Jesus, Jesus, how I trust him! How I've proved him o'er and o'er!
Jesus, Jesus, precious Jesus! O for grace to trust him more!

WORDS: Louisa M. R. Stead, 1882

26

Dementia I

IN THE PRELUDE OF MY MEMOIR, I mentioned that my mother suffered from dementia, most likely it was Alzheimer's disease. This dreaded disease is named after a German physician who first described it as a progressive, irreversible disease characterized by degeneration of the brain cells and commonly leading to severe dementia. Interestingly, one dictionary defines dementia synonymously with insanity or madness. The school of Psychiatry is a little gentler in its description of this dreaded disease saying it is, "… a progressive neurodegenerative condition. It is one of the most common forms of dementia, a group of symptoms that lead to a decline in mental function severe enough to disrupt daily life. Alzheimer's causes problems with a person's memory and ability to learn, reason, make judgments, communicate and carry out daily activities."[9] Regardless of how it is described, it is an insidious disease.

There is dementia on my mother's side of the family, and it has affected some of her other relatives. On my father's side… well, my grandmother lived to be one hundred and one, and my dad lived beyond the age of ninety-one. My brother and I agree that we'll probably live to be a hundred, but… we won't know about it.

I share this topic of dementia with you, the reader, because of a humorous story concerning my mother. Her dementia started making its ugly appearance while she was in her early eighties. I was the senior pastor at the Willowbrook UMC in Sun City, and she was aware that something was interfering with her thought processes. During the times she and my father would fly over to visit us from San Diego, she would remark, "I hate this." She was referring, of course, to her inability to remember who she was and who other persons were; especially persons in her life that loved her the most.

During such times, I would put my arm around her, kiss her on the forehead, and say, "Mom, don't worry about it. You're a child of God, beloved in his sight; and we love you, too. You belong to us, and we belong to you. It's going to be all right." If this assurance ever brought her any comfort, I don't know. However, it brought a kind of peace with me in my attempt to encourage her.

In 1999, my mother was approaching her eighty-fourth birthday. Nevertheless, when the subject was brought up, she would insist that she was going to be eighty-two! My father would say, "No, honey. You're going to be eighty-four."

"I am not!" she would angrily respond. "Don't tell me how old I'm going to be! I'm going to be eighty-two!"

Whenever the subject of her age came up, it was like walking on eggshells. Mom stubbornly insisted that she was going to be eighty-two.

Well, her birthday in June came and went. Father's Day was a couple of weeks later, and I called my Dad. I wished him a happy day, and we chatted for a short time. Before closing the call, I said to him, "Let me talk to Mom."

Now, I'm the eldest child in our family. Moreover, I know how to push my mother's buttons, so to speak. She came to the telephone, and we talked briefly. Then I asked, "Well, Mom, how old are you now?"

Her response was immediate. "Well, they say I'm eighty-four, but I think I'm eighty-two!"

I said, "Okay. What year were you born?"

Again, her response was quick. "1915!"

I replied, "Okay. However, when I subtract 1915 from 1999, I get 84. Mom, the math says you're eighty-four!"

She was quiet for a few moments, and I guessed that maybe Mom was trying to do the math in her head.

However, before she could respond, I said, "Come on, Mom. We've got to get this straightened out because the people in my congregation aren't going to understand why I was two years old when you and Dad finally got married!"

With this, my mother started laughing. I mean, she got the giggles. Our telephone conversation ended her insistence on being younger by two years.

The following year, when I called her on her birthday and asked, "How old are you now, Mom?"

She answered impatiently, "Eighty-five!"

The year after that, when I called and asked the same question, she responded as if talking to a forgetful child, "Why, Jimmy, you ought to know that by now. I'm eighty-six."

The next year, though, Mom couldn't remember her age. Then, in September, my parents celebrated their sixty-fifth wedding anniversary. A party was held at the home of my younger brother. Many family members were present, and Mom remarked to my wife, Martha, "I don't know who all these people are, but I know they belong to me."

At the conclusion of the party, my father took my mother to a care center where she lived the last six months of her life. During this time, Mom seemed to withdraw into herself. She would press her chin onto her chest and wouldn't look at anyone. When I attempted to lift her chin, Mom resisted. She refused to talk except... when I started reading familiar biblical passages. Then, she would join me. When Martha and I would sing some of the old, familiar hymns, Mom would sing along with us. The words of scripture and song were still there in the recesses of her mind, and for a while, the mother that I knew came forth like a Lazarus from the tomb.

Does the possibility of my contracting Alzheimer's disease or any form of dementia frighten me? No, not at all. Though my memory of a loving mother and father is something I hold dear, how long these remembrances and others I cherish will exist, who knows? At this moment in my life, I do remember Paul's words of encouragement to the church members in Rome:

> *I consider that the sufferings of this present time are not worth comparing with the glory about to be revealed to us ... We know that all things work together for good for those who love God, who are called according to his purpose ... What then are we to say about these things? If God is for us, who is against us? ... No, in all these things we are more than*

*conquerors through him who loved us. For I am convinced that neither death, nor life, nor angels, nor rulers, nor things present, nor things to come, nor powers, nor height, nor depth, nor anything else in all creation, will be able to separate us from the love of God in Christ Jesus our Lord. (*Romans 8: 28, 31, 37-39.)

I have always been strengthened by the perfect love of God that casts out fear. About death, I have no fear.

Now Thank We All Our God

Now thank we all our God, with heart and hands and voices,
who wondrous things has done, in whom this world rejoices;
who from our mother's arms has blessed us on our way
with countless gifts of love, and still is ours today.
WORDS: Martin Rinkart, 1663; trans. By Catherine Winkworth, 1858

27

Dementia II

I AM ADDING ANOTHER STORY to the previous one because of a film Martha and I saw sometime in March of 2015. The film, "Still Alice," is based on a true story written by Lisa Genova. At the time of this writing, the film is still being shown in several movie theaters. The main character, Alice Howland, is portrayed by the very talented actress Julianne Moore. By coincidence, my mother's name was Julia Ann.

Alice Howland was a professor at Harvard University with a doctorate in psychology. She taught courses in cognitive psychology for twenty-five years, did research in the field of linguistics, and lectured all over the world. She was diagnosed with early-onset Alzheimer's disease somewhere around the age of fifty.

The film, especially Alice's speech to a group of persons involved in the research and treatment of Alzheimer's, was especially moving to me since, as previously stated, I have some medical history with this form of dementia and carry its genes through my mother's side of the family.

I wept while listening to Alice's speech. I thought of my mom who had, in the words of Alice, "… no control over which yesterdays I keep and which ones get deleted." My mother lost the memories she had of my father, her three children, and nine grandchildren. She didn't know who we were and we, all of us, felt her frustration and confusion.

Following the film and as Martha and I headed toward our car, she asked me, "Do you think you would like to know?"

I responded, "I think I would."

A week later, while visiting my primary care physician on unrelated concerns, I brought up the film we had seen and told my doctor that I wanted to gather information regarding the testing procedures for Alzheimer's. He asked if I wanted a referral to a neurologist, and I replied, "Yes."

I have since seen this neurologist, and he gave me some helpful information and advice. Apparently, the single-gene mutations directly responsible for early-onset Alzheimer's disease (which my mother did not have) do not seem to be involved in late-onset Alzheimer's (which is what my mom experienced).

Moreover, although a blood test can identify which Apolipoprotein E (APOE) gene and which forms or alleles a person has, it cannot predict who will or will not develop Alzheimer's disease. The material I received said, "It is unlikely that genetic testing will ever be able to predict the disease with 100 percent accuracy because too many other factors may influence its development and progression." Of course, there's much more information on the topic, but I'll not involve you, dear reader, in the complicated medical details and jargon.

My conclusion: There is no reason to be concerned about the testing procedure. The cost for the testing, called Admark Early-Onset Alzheimer's Evaluation, is steep, and it's unlikely that my health insurance would be involved. Therefore, I'm not going to worry myself about any future possibilities of the disease disrupting my life and the lives of those I love best. I will continue to trust God with my life and with my death and all the time I have to enjoy God's, undeserved love. Here's the third verse of this beloved hymn:

I'll Praise My Maker While I've Breath
The Lord pours eyesight on the blind; the Lord supports the
fainting mind and sends the laboring conscience peace.
God helps the stranger in distress, the widow and the fatherless,
and grants the prisoner sweet release.
WORDS: Isaac Watts, 1719; alt. by John Wesley, 1737 (Ps. 146)

28

Contemplation

IN ANTHONY DOERR'S beautiful novel, *All the Light We Cannot See,* he gives a poignant description of how we all come into being, how we enter into the wondrous gift of life. He writes these poetic words[10]:

> We all come into existence as a single cell, smaller than a speck of dust. Much smaller. Divide. Multiply. Add and subtract. Matter changes hands, atoms flow in and out, molecules pivot, proteins stitch together, mitochondria sends out their oxidative dictates; we begin as a microscopic electrical swarm. Forty weeks later, six trillion cells get crushed in the vise of our mother's birth canal, and we howl. Then the world starts in on us.

Reread these words, this time out loud. Aren't they marvelous? Oh, to be able to write in this fashion.

For those of us who adhere to Judeo-Christian values, a term used since the 1950s to encompass the prevailing ethical standards of Judaism and Christianity, several other authors reflect the same beautiful flow of words in their poetry and prose. I'm specifically talking about the book of Psalms.

Biblical scholars state that Psalms in its present form is the product of the post-exilic community of Israel. It is commonly referred to as the Psalter and spoken of as "the hymnbook of the second Temple."

The Psalter and its process of completion took place in several stages, extending from about the fourth to the second centuries BCE. It is composed of five collections or books, each of which concludes with a doxology (a hymn of praise to God). The number five also corresponds to the first five books of the Hebrew Bible called *Torah* or the Pentateuch, meaning "the law." It's interesting that Matthew, who wrote his gospel to persuade Jews of the authenticity of Jesus as the Messiah, structures the Sermon on the Mount as a five-part discourse.

Whoa… I digress. Moreover, I'm starting to sound like a seminary professor. Sorry. What I want to do is contemplate and compare Doerr's quotation with one of my favorite psalms, Psalm 8:1-9. Here are the words of the psalmist:

> *O LORD, our Sovereign, how majestic is your name in all the earth!*
> *When I look at your heavens, the work of your fingers, the moon and the stars that you have established; what are human beings that you are mindful of them, mortals that you care for them?*
> *Yet you have made them a little lower than God (Or than divine beings or angels), and crowned them with glory and honor.*
> *You have given them dominion over the works of your hands; you have put all things under their feet, all sheep and oxen, and also the beasts of the field, the birds of the air, and the fish of the sea, whatever passes along the paths of the seas.*
> *O LORD, our sovereign, how majestic is your name in all the earth!*

I invite you to contemplate with me. This is the first hymn of praise in the Psalter. Moreover, it is the only hymn in the entire Old Testament composed wholly as a direct address to God. Though a portion of this Psalm acknowledges the finiteness of a human being, our unimportance, and limits, it also stresses how much God cares for us.

For the follower of Jesus, I think Psalm 8 has special meaning, especially when reinterpreted in the light of the Christ. We hold a special place in the heart of God. We are the object of God's affection. You and I are God's children. We have value. We are important. We are loved. No one is excluded. Every one of us (non-Christians, too)!

As those who, in Christ, recognize the worth of every human being, when we praise the LORD with this psalm, we do so in contrition and hope, remembering that "...the creation waits with eager longing for the revealing of the children of God" (Romans 8:18).

What Wondrous Love Is This

What wondrous love is this, O my soul, O my soul,
whatwondrous love is this, O my soul!
What wondrous love is this that caused the Lord of bliss to bear
the dreadful curse for my soul, for my soul,
to bear the dreadful curse for my soul.

WORDS: Text first published in 1811

29

The Burning

DURING A RECENT TRIP TO SAN DIEGO to visit our son and his family, I was reminded of something I experienced some forty plus years ago. I was relatively new as the pastor of the congregation at Trinity UMC in Yuma, Arizona. A retreat event for United Methodist Men was held at one of our conference camps, Pine Canyon, in the Chiricahua Mountains south of Tucson, a beautiful setting for spiritual inspiration and relaxation.

To get to our destination from Yuma, we traveled Interstate 8 east to Gila Bend and then southeast to Tucson. We had two carloads of men from our church attending the retreat. Both cars were equipped with CB (Citizens' Band) radios, and we kept in communication with each other while traveling. I don't recall much of what happened at the retreat. I do remember that it was designed for laymen and not ordained pastors, so I felt a little out of place. The thing I mainly recall is something that happened on the way home.

The driver of the car in which I was riding was Joe Neff. Joe was a citrus farmer and member of our church. Originally from Texas or one of the southern states, Joe had a definite southern twang. Somewhere south of Gila Bend, Joe must have been driving a little too fast. All of a sudden, an Arizona Highway patrol car flashed its lights at us. Joe had been talking to the driver of our other car when this occurred. He exclaimed over the CB radio, "Uh-oh, I've been had!"

After pulling over to the side of the road, the patrolman approached our car. Joe rolled down his window and proceeded to get his driver's license and registration. The officer's first words were, "Uh-oh, you've been had!" He had been listening to Joe's conversation on his CB radio. Fortunately, the officer let Joe off with a warning to slow it down.

We passed through the small town of Gila Bend and soon, off in the distance, we could see a large, black column of smoke. As we got nearer, the intensity of the smoke grew larger until eventually, we saw the cause. A car had flipped over in the median strip and was burning. Inside the burning car, we could see the blurred figure of a person. Some other vehicles had stopped, and people were standing around watching helplessly. Emergency vehicles had not yet arrived. Though it was a shocking sight, there wasn't anything we could do but drive on.

After we had got back to Yuma, we learned the next day that the other car traveling with us had stopped at the scene of the accident. One of the men in our group noticed an elderly couple among the onlookers. The woman was crying. The man explained that the form in the car was their daughter-in-law. They were returning from San Diego where their son, a sailor in the U.S. Navy, had just deployed for a nine-month cruise aboard his ship. His wife was driving their car back, and they were following her. Apparently, she fell asleep at the wheel, and when the vehicle veered off the shoulder of the highway, she woke up abruptly and turned the steering wheel sharply, thus causing the automobile to flip over. It caught fire immediately.

How tragic! Can you imagine the helplessness of her in-laws? Can you feel their horror, pain and anguish, and sadness? Do you wonder how they could get word to their son of his wife's death? And their son… Who would notify him? Where would his ship be and how would he get back home to make funeral arrangements for his beloved? How long had they been married? Were any children involved in their marriage? These and other questions haunted me. I was sorry our car made the decision not to stop. I was glad our other car took the time and was present to give some measure of comfort to the elderly couple.

Now, for the past forty years plus, every time we pass this spot on the highway, approximately two to three miles east of the little community of Sentinel/Agua Caliente, I remember that dark form in the burning car and relive the scene in my mind. I can't forget. I don't want to forget.

James D. Wood

Pass Me Not, O Gentle Savior

Pass me not, O gentle Savior, hear my humble cry;
while on others thou art calling, do not pass me by.
Savior, Savior, hear my humble cry;
while on others thou art calling, do not pass me by.

WORDS: Fanny J. Crosby, 1868

30

The Saddle

SOMETIME DURING THE SUMMER of 2014, my wife and I participated in a Bed and Breakfast vacation. I use the term vacation loosely because when you're retired, every day could be considered as such. Our friends in England refer to this time away from the usual daily routine as a holiday. This terminology doesn't seem to fit the lifestyle of most Americans and, actually, the English (and European) use of the word holiday appears to be a misnomer as it originally meant Holy Day.

Again, I digress (I do more of this the older I get). Our time away was spent in southern Arizona at the Spirit Tree Inn, located in the small community of Patagonia. Patagonia is a very picturesque area situated about an hour's drive south of Tucson. The location, because of its higher elevation, is known for growing several varieties of grapes—grapes used in the making of wine by several commercial wineries.

The Spirit of Tree Inn turned out to be a delightful place for a quiet respite. For reasons unknown to us, Martha and I were the only clientele at this particular time and had the entire facility to ourselves. The caretaker of the property on which the large home was situated also served as the cook, and each morning he prepared a delicious and nutritious breakfast for us.

Besides the numerous animals that resided at the Spirit of Tree Inn— cats, dogs, horses, chickens, and mules—the area was known for more than three hundred species of birds that were attracted to the Patagonia area. At other times during the year, mainly springtime, many bird watchers came to reside for a while at the Inn.

Here's one of my favorite pieces of Arizona trivia, and it relates to Patagonia and the surrounding area. The movie "Oklahoma" was filmed here. When Curly McLain sang about the "bright golden haze on the meadow," he did it in this part of Arizona. Apparently, the filmmakers couldn't find enough undeveloped land in the Sooner State, so they chose the windswept grasslands of Santa Cruz County as a more suitable location. Other classic movies with roots in the area include "The Outlaw Josie Wales," "A Star Is Born," "Hombre," "Pork Chop Hill," and "The Big Country."

Moreover, an hour's drive from Patagonia is the famous Old Western town of Tombstone. Many books and films have been dedicated to telling the story of Wyatt Earp, his brothers, and Doc Holliday and the gunfight at the O.K. Corral. With this in mind, one of our mornings we decided to make the drive and revisit Tombstone.

After arriving, Martha and I took a tour of the town on an old stagecoach. We saw places we had not seen before, and our driver was quite adept at retelling some of Tombstone's history. As we passed the Old Courthouse, now a museum, he encouraged us to visit it and acquire some more knowledge of its historical significance. We agreed that it was something we might be interested in doing.

The Old Courthouse was very compelling in portraying a broader picture of Tombstone's history. On the second floor, among all the exhibits, was a saddle strapped onto a metal frame. A sign near it read, "Warning: Use at Your Own Risk!" I thought to myself, *Hmm. What would be risky about using a stationary saddle?* I soon found out.

Placing my left foot in the stirrup and grabbing the saddle horn, I swung up onto the saddle. No problem. I started clowning around for my wife's benefit, making clicking sounds and slapping my right hip as though I were riding on a real Cayuse (that's a small Western horse used by cowboys to you greenhorns). I started singing (there was no one else around, mind you) a few lines of "Don't Fence Me In," but Martha was unimpressed. Embarrassed might be a better word. She's very patient and long-suffering when it comes to some of my antics. Well, perhaps not that long-suffering. Shortly, she encouraged me to "unstraddle my old saddle" because time was wasting. Coming back to reality, I shrugged and swung off the saddle—very fast!

This time, my body weight, combined with the momentum of my swing, caused my left foot to go under the saddle and bam! I landed on my back, hard! My head hit the wooden floor with a loud thud! Ouch!

I was stunned for a few seconds. I heard Martha exclaim, "Oh, Jim!" Downstairs, the woman employee of the Courthouse Museum yelled, "Is everything all right up there?"

I was able to respond, "I think so." But everything wasn't. I hurt badly.

The drive back to Patagonia and the Spirit of Tree Inn was painful. That night—our last night, thankfully—I didn't sleep well. Every time I turned over in bed, my back hurt. The next day, Martha called my chiropractor in Chandler and made an appointment for me later that same day. It took several sessions before the back pain dissolved completely. I can laugh today, whenever I tell this story, but it wasn't funny then… the day I was thrown by a saddle!

Abide with Me
Abide with me; fast falls the eventide;
the darkness deepens; Lord, with me abide.
When other helpers fail and comforts flee,
Help of the helpless, O abide with me.
WORDS: Henry F. Lyte, 1847 (Lk. 24:29)

31

2041

2041. THIS IS THE YEAR SOME predict the end of religion as we know it today, the "some" being Sam Harris and Richard Dawkins. Both are anti-theists, a more intense form of atheism (those who are convinced that God doesn't exist) and agnostics (those who don't know for sure whether or not God exists). A Religion News Service (RNS) poll reveals that anti-theists compose fifteen percent of atheists.[11]

Harris has written a book, *End of Faith*, espousing his beliefs. In it, Harris concludes that the events surrounding the 9/11 terrorist attacks make it necessary to rid the world of all religion. Dawkins, in his book *The God Delusion*, asks his readers to "Imagine, with John Lennon, a world with no religion. Imagine no suicide bombers, no 9/11, no Crusades, no Inquisition, no witch hunts … no shiny-suited bouffant-haired televangelists fleecing gullible people of their money."[12] I could easily imagine a world without the negative connotations of religion where its adherents worship the false idols of materialism, greed, and power. Yes, I could.

However, let's also try to imagine a world without Martin Luther King, Jr. and Gandhi. What would the world be like without church soup kitchens, homeless shelters, and hospitals started by various Catholic and Protestant groups? Perhaps anti-theists can envision the absence of faith-based efforts to fight Ebola, malaria, sex trafficking, and the ISIS genocide. But I can't. I can't imagine a world without God believers, who far out-give anti-theists to help refugees from famine, wars, and natural disasters.

If you can be so imaginative, how about reinventing a world without the atheistic leadership of Joseph Stalin, Pol Pot, and Hitler. Of course, the truth is that evil will exist with or without religion because sick people will always find a way to pursue their agenda of hate.

In another recent Religion News Service article, it reports that the United States is a significantly less Christian country than it was seven years ago (2007 vs. 2014). Though Christianity still dominates American religious identity (70 percent), the survey shows dramatic shifts as more people move out the doors of denominations, shedding spiritual connections along the way.

Atheists and agnostics, also referred to as "nones," have nearly doubled their share of the religious marketplace. Atheists rose from 1.6 percent to 3.1 percent, and agnostics from 2.4 to 4.0 percent. There are more "nones" than Evangelical Lutherans, United Methodists, and Episcopalians combined. Apparently, the official motto of the United States which was adopted in 1956 (the same year I graduated from high school), "In God We Trust," is diminishing in importance.

So what does all this mean to me and why am I writing this piece? I see some of the above trends in the lives of those I love best—my children and grandchildren. Though Martha and I have attempted to be faith influential in their lives, especially as they were growing up, that encouragement has not had the lasting effect we had hoped.

Don't misunderstand, they are righteous, moralistic persons. They have done a fantastic job raising their children. What is missing; however, is the guidance and strength a community of faith provides through its nurture, spiritual resources, and unselfish concern for others.

I don't know, maybe we're the last or next to the last generation that centers its living on God through Jesus the Christ. Or, perhaps the younger generations have focused on our failures and weaknesses, and our occasional hypocrisy in being the people of God. Or, maybe our children, having grown up in the church, made the decision that enough is enough. But their children have not had the exposure to the gifts and graces provided through the church and, therefore, have no basis for their ignorance of the Christian faith. It was Søren Kierkegaard, the Danish existentialist philosopher and theologian, who wrote:

There are two ways to be fooled. One is to believe what isn't true; the other is to refuse to believe what is true.

I share what truth I have come to believe. Throughout this writing, I have referred to some hymns and scripture. Some in my family may never know the strength and inner peace their words provide. Some may never experience the sheer joy that comes from helping others, whether it's participating in a Hunger Walk or working on a Habitat for Humanity home. Whether its preparing and serving meals for homeless families or being involved in a mission project that helps people who literally have none of the comforts most of us in this country enjoy and take for granted.

Some of those I love may never come to know what trust in a loving power beyond our limited understanding, a force more clearly defined by a man from Galilee more than two thousand years ago, can bring to everyday living. That man, Jesus of Nazareth, whom we believe to be the Messiah (Jewish title), the Christ (Greek title), and God's anointed one, through his life, teachings, healings, compassion for others, death, and resurrection has provided forgiveness for our wrong-doings, strength for difficult life situations, purposeful living, and hope for that which is beyond death.

Or, they may come to know this truth in their lives. I hope they do. After all, God's not through with any of us yet.

Faith of Our Fathers

Faith of our fathers, living still,
in spite of dungeon, fire, and sword;
O how our hearts beat high with joy
when e'er we hear that glorious word!
Faith of our fathers, holy faith!
We will be true to thee till death.

WORDS: Frederick W. Faber, 1849

32

Life Abundant

IN THE GOSPEL ACCORDING TO JOHN, the Evangelist takes us behind the scenes of Jesus' ministry, giving us a glimpse into his eternal origin and divine nature. Though the author records real events, he goes beyond them in interpreting these events. In other words, John is engaging in theology while symbolically using some terms drawn from everyday experience—bread, water, light, life, word, shepherd, door, and way—to make the understanding of Christ both clear and compelling.

In Chapter 10, verses 1 through 10, John describes Jesus as the Good Shepherd, the One who knows his flock by name and who trust and follow him because they know his voice. To further explain his understanding of Jesus, John uses a literary device in verse 6:

> *Jesus used this figure of speech with them (his listeners),*
> *but they did not understand what he was saying to them.*

John continues with these words of scripture:

> *So again Jesus said to them, "Very truly, I tell you, I am the*
> *gate for the sheep. All who came before me (false prophets)*
> *are thieves and bandits; but the sheep did not listen to them.*
> *I am the gate. Whoever enters by me will be saved, and will*
> *come in and go out and find pasture. The thief comes only*
> *to steal and kill and destroy. I came that they may have life,*
> *and have it abundantly." (John 10:7-10.)*

The General Board of Pension and Health Benefits of The United Methodist Church recently released (2015) the results of its Clergy Health Survey Report. It reached out to 4,000 UMC clergy; however, only 38 percent responded. I'm sure the rest must have thought, as I did when engaged in full-time ministry work, "I don't have time to fill out another stupid survey!"

Nevertheless, of those who filled out the 100-question online survey, these key findings were revealed:

- 42 percent of respondents are currently obese—a much higher percentage than a demographically matched sample of U.S. adults (37 percent).
- 49 percent have "ever had" high cholesterol at some point—also much higher than the comparable benchmark of 16 percent.
- 35 percent have "ever had" high blood pressure at some point—again, higher than the comparable benchmark of 20 percent.
- 7 percent suffer from depression as measured by frequency of depressive symptoms—more than twice that of the similar reference.
- 25 percent of UMC clergy experienced stress as a result of dealing with ministry personnel who are critical of them.
- And finally, 46 percent of UMC clergy experienced at least one intrusive ministry demand (devotion to ministry questioned, doubts about the pastor's faith, and so forth).

Ah, now perhaps the reader can see where this chapter is headed. As persons who have been schooled, examined and declared fit and ready for ministry, ordained and set apart as leaders in The United Methodist Church, what's wrong with this picture? Does this sound like the promise of Jesus, that "I came that they may have life, and have it abundantly," is being fulfilled in the lives of our clergy?

Though I am not obese (overweight by ten pounds, maybe), I have experienced some of the above health problems. Consultation with medical professionals and prescriptions have brought me back into a healthy arena. Moreover, much of the above symptoms diminished once I reached the retired relationship. Helpful, too, has been a regimen of exercise at local fitness centers. My positive outlook on life and desire to pay it forward through community volunteerism has been a high factor in a healthy mental and spiritual attitude. Of course, all this could change in the twinkling of an eye. Nevertheless, I find myself in a good place right now. I am experiencing the life of which our Lord spoke, and it is good!

Rejoice, Ye Pure in Heart

Rejoice, ye pure in heart; give thanks, and sing;
your glorious banner wave on high, the cross of Christ your King.
Rejoice, (rejoice), rejoice, (rejoice),
give thanks and sing.
WORDS: Edward H. Plumptre, 1865 (Ps. 20:4; 147:1; Phil. 4:4)

33

Yard Work

FOR MOST OF MY LIFE, I have performed the chore of cutting the grass, edging the lawn, trimming bushes, weeding the flower bed—in short, doing the yard work.

This work routine, usually done weekly, began when I was a boy growing up in Pacific Beach (the north shore bay area of San Diego) in a Federal Housing Project named Bayview Terrace. Though we didn't have much lawn, part of my chores or responsibilities for the yard included cleaning up after my duck and our Irish Setter dog (think feces here for both pets). This was in addition to washing/drying dishes, babysitting my siblings, and polishing the family's shoes on Saturday night in preparation for Sunday school and church. For this, I received twenty-five cents a week. It was enough.

To supplement my meager income, I would canvass the neighborhood Saturday afternoons and mow lawns for twenty-five cents. This revenue would enable me to buy comic books, purchase model airplane kits, and attend Saturday morning matinees at the Roxy Theater each week.

My junior/senior high school years were the same. I was responsible for the yard work—and more! Things didn't change once I got married. Oh, I had a brief respite during our son's junior/senior high school years, but once he left home for college ... the yard work resumed.

When I was involved in full-time ministry work as a pastor, I looked forward to my day off, usually Wednesday. Why? That was the day to spend the entire morning doing lots of ... yard work! You see, I was spending a lot of my time sitting behind a desk, sitting behind the wheel of my car, sitting in church meetings, sitting in a hospital room, sitting ... you get the point. In other words, I was exercising my brain and mind but not my body. But doing yard work reminded my body that it, too, had a function. The muscles would be sore, my heart rate would soar (notice the play on words here), I would sweat profusely, I would get tired and need an occasional rest, and I would sleep well at night. Moreover, during this time, I would pray for others and work on sermon ideas. I felt closer to God and came to look at yard work as relaxing, spiritual therapy!

Even in retirement, I enjoyed the healthy benefits of yard work ... until recently. I noticed all my neighbors, save one, were hiring yard work people, mostly Hispanics. I resisted for eleven years into retirement, but I finally succumbed. The summer heat in the Sonoran desert (think 117 degrees) wore me out. Now our yard landscaper and his crew do this monthly chore for me. It's well worth it to pay them and besides, I now have the opportunity to practice my Spanish!

In the Garden

I come to the garden alone while the dew is still on the roses,
and the voice I hear falling on my ear, the Son of God discloses.
And he walks with me, and he talks with me,
and he tells me I am his own;
and the joy we share as we tarry there, none other has ever known.
WORDS: C. Austin Miles, 1913 (John 20:11-18)

⮌ 34 ⮍

Estate Planning

SEVERAL YEARS BEFORE RETIREMENT, Martha and I contacted an attorney to help us plan our wills and living trust agreement. We selected one who was recommended by our Annual Conference's Foundation. Our attorney developed a good, sound portfolio, which included the power of attorney stipulations and revocable trust, for a very reasonable fee. We felt our assets were protected and safe, and in the event of our deaths, our beneficiaries would know our wishes exactly.

Then about nine years into retirement, we were notified that our attorney was retiring. It was suggested that we update our financial and health portfolio with another attorney. I contacted the Conference office for suggestions. I was referred to a lawyer whose office was in the eastern part of Mesa, Arizona, about ten to fifteen miles from our home.

We met with the attorney for a consultation. After updating our portfolio information with him, he stated that the cost would be approximately twelve hundred dollars. This was about three hundred dollars more than our original portfolio price, and the update included more safeguards, so it seemed reasonable enough.

With the bulk of the work done on our part, I engaged our new attorney in some small talk. I asked if he and his family were involved in a United Methodist church. I thought he might be since our Conference office had recommended him.

He responded, "Why, yes. We're members of the Gold Canyon United Methodist Church."

Martha and I looked at each other. I smiled and said to our attorney, "I'm the pastor who started that church."

He brightened and said, "Really!" Then he enthusiastically told us how he and his family happened to pass by the church one Sunday evening. He had two children, both youth age, and they saw members of the church's youth group playing outside the building. They stopped and chatted with the youth counselors while their children were greeted warmly and welcomed by the church youth. The family attended, joined the church, and have been worshiping there ever since.

The story was heartwarming (John Wesley isn't the only one to have this experience). Martha and I left the attorney's office and would return in a couple of weeks to sign the documents. When we did, and after completing all the forms with our signatures, I pulled out our checkbook to make payment.

Mr. Sheridan put up his hand saying, "There's no charge. You are the founding pastor of the church we love so much, and that loves us in return. Thank you!"

I gulped. Tears came to Martha's eyes. We were speechless except to extend our own gratitude. We left feeling very amazed … and thankful.

Trust and Obey
When we walk with the Lord in the light of his word,
what a glory he sheds on our way!
While we do his good will, he abides with us still,
and with all who will trust and obey.
Trust and obey, for there's no other way
to be happy in Jesus, but to trust and obey.
WORDS: John H. Sammis, 1887 (Jn. 1:7)

ᔰ 35 ᔱ

I Wonder...

IN ONE OF FREDERICK BUECHNER'S books, he writes this poignant piece[13]:

> *There is a sad and dangerous little game that people play when they get to be a certain age. It is a form of solitaire. They get out their class yearbook, and look at the pictures of classmates they knew best and recall the days when they first knew them in school, ten or twenty years ago or whatever it was. They think about all the exciting, crazy, wonderfully characteristic things their classmates used to be interested in and about the dreams they had about what they were going to do when they graduated and about the kind of dreams that maybe they had for some of them. Then they think about what those classmates actually did with their lives, what they are doing with them now ten or twenty years later.*

Buechner makes no claim that this game is always sad, but the once or twice when he played it, sadness has been a large part of what he felt. I have played this little game several times in my life, especially more so during my years of retirement. Though the emotion of sadness has been present, a prevailing sense of wonderment has been dominant. With this in mind, I want to share some of my innermost thoughts prefaced by the phrase, "I wonder..."

114

I wonder how my life would have been different had my parents not moved from Nebraska when I was about three years old. I would not have met my soulmate, Martha; our two oldest children would not have been born; our youngest daughter, whom we adopted, would not have been part of our family.

I wonder how the lives of my boyhood chums turned out… Darrell, Larry, Dennis, and Stevie. I know what happened to my best friend, Jackie. He turned out to be a gay man and, in despair, took his own life. Dennis, I discovered recently, died in 2014 at the age of 76. But the others…

I wonder what happened to my favorite schoolteacher when I was in the sixth grade, Mr. Lucas. Where did he go after Bayview Terrace Elementary was closed to make way for the development of Capehart Navy Housing?

I wonder what my life would have been like had my parents not moved to National City following my first year in junior high school. I would have eventually attended La Jolla High School with the future Raquel Welch. Hmmm.

I wonder about my spiritual development had my parents not decided to change churches from Presbyterian to Methodist. I would not have met my best high school friend, John. Moreover, I would not have asked my future wife, "Do you have a ride home? No? Well, you do now!"

I wonder about my favorite, eccentric, but extremely effective high school English teacher, Mrs. Stone. What happened to her after I graduated? I regret not going back to Sweetwater High and telling her how much I appreciated her influence on my life.

I wonder about the direction my life would have taken had I not flunked out of San Diego State College my first semester. Would I have continued my efforts to be a fraternity member of Lambda Chi Alpha? Do I have any regrets about this lesson producing experience? Absolutely not!

I wonder about the events during the summer of 1965 when I was wrestling with making a decision about ordained ministry. What if my fears had prevailed? They were great, and I was scared. What if I had not listened to or ignored God's call? That would have been the biggest mistake of my life.

I wonder what would have happened if I had chosen another seminary to attend. I would not have had the benefit of being the student pastor of a loving congregation. We would not have been in a place where the adoption of our youngest daughter occurred.

I wonder about my first appointment to a local church after seminary. I was slated to go to a church in San Diego but went to a larger church in Long Beach. The senior pastor with whom I would work was my former district superintendent. He was influential in my being approved for final ordination. Another indication of God's preceding grace.

I don't wonder about the churches to which we were appointed. Each provided experiences to love and be loved in return. Each offered difficulties to be resolved and joys to be savored. We met so many caring and appreciative persons that assisted our growth as travelers on the journey of faith. Each congregation was a delight, especially as we neared the retired relationship.

Nor do I wonder about our choice of a faith community after retirement. We are happy and content in Sun Lakes. We have a close circle of friends, we enjoy the opportunities the church and larger community offers to pay it forward, to share the blessings of God by being a blessing to others.

I do wonder about our children, grandchildren, and great-granddaughters. Will they have the spiritual stamina and resources to meet head-on the inevitable problems of life? A seminary professor of mine was fond of saying, "When we encounter life's difficulties we either grow up or fold up." I wonder if my loved ones will have this kind of toughness that relies on God.

As I have grown older and more dependent upon the skills and knowledge of those in the medical professions, there is something that often comes uninvited into my mind. I wonder when my life as I know it will end. I wonder how it will end. I wonder at what age it will end. These wonderings are not accompanied by any fear of the unknown. There is, instead, a peaceful curiosity about them. It will be a new experience for me, one that everyone has and will experience, one that is inevitable, and a mystery yet to be revealed.

I happened to come across an interesting comment in a novel written by Daniel Silva. About one of the main characters, he writes[14]:

> *She was one of the few people on the island who knew the truth about him. She knew his long litany of sins and misdeeds*

and even claimed to know the time and circumstances of his death. It was the one thing she refused to tell him. "It is not my place," she would whisper to him in her candlelit parlor. "Besides, to know how life ends would only ruin the story."

We can try to turn the pages of our lives to the end of the story to see how it ends, but this is an impossible task. It is the hope of the faithful; however, that the ending will be a beautiful surprise—a surprise that does not ruin the story but instead makes it complete.

I'll conclude with a hymn I've already referenced, but use the fourth stanza:

There's a Wideness in God's Mercy

If our love were but more simple, we should rest upon God's word;
and our lives would be illumined by the presence of our Lord.

WORDS: Frederick W. Faber, 1854

36

The Prophet

DURING THE 1960s COUNTERCULTURE ERA (think "Hippy"), a book published in 1923 became very popular. The author was Kahlil Gibran, and the book was *The Prophet*. Gibran was born January 6, 1883, into a Maronite Catholic family from the historical town of Bsharri in northern Mount Lebanon, then a semi-autonomous part of the Ottoman Empire. As a young man, he immigrated with his family to the United States, where he studied art and began his literary career, writing both in English and Arabic. Though he was known as a poet, painter, philosopher, theologian, and visual artist, he is chiefly known in the English-speaking world for *The Prophet*, an early example of inspirational fiction including a series of philosophical essays written in English poetic prose. Gibran died April 10, 1931, at the age of forty-eight.[15]

Portions of Gibran's essays, notably those on *Children*, *Marriage*, and *Death*, were often used by clergy in sermons, wedding ceremonies, and funerals. I have probably quoted some of Gibran's prose myself, possibly during the 1970s, though I have no specific recollection.

Why, the reader may ask, have I decided to write about this subject? Why have I included a remembrance about a book long forgotten by those now preoccupied with acquiring material things in the twenty-first century, a world so fascinated and absorbed with technological achievements?

Did you know that Gibran is the third best-selling poet of all time, behind Shakespeare and Lao Tzu (or Laozi), a philosopher and poet of ancient China? Remember, China has almost five times the population of the United States. However, that's not in the equation for writing this piece. No, a less than significant factor is that a movie, an animated film no less, was recently released on *The Prophet*. Martha and I, along with friends, saw this beautifully adapted 2014 film and were impressed. Produced by Salma Hayek, the actress who was also part of the voice cast, the striking visuals and music elevated verses that I had forgotten. Other voices in the film include well-known actors such as Liam Neeson, Alfred Molina, and Frank Langella. I encourage the reader to see this captivating movie.

The book and film stirred the recesses in my memory and recalled another book, this one written by an ordained minister in the Reformed Church in America (RCA), William Martin. Bill is married to one of our United Methodist clergy and together they have led a variety of retreats around our country. I attended one of these several years ago and purchased his book, *The Art of Pastoring: Contemplative Reflections.*

Bill uses the style of Lao Tzu (mentioned previously) in disseminating his wisdom for pastors. I have found his book very helpful and enlightening. I will only share one essence of thought or reflection as most reading this will not identify, unless you are a preacher, with its resonating insight. Someone once wrote, "Being a pastor is like being a stray dog at a whistler's convention." Funny, but mostly to those of us privileged to serve congregations in an ordained capacity. Oh, well.

Bill cautions the pastor about filling in his/her days with "busyness"— things that come with the vocation of ministry, such as appointments, church meetings, budget concerns, and administrative problems—but distract from time with God and persons in need. He emphasizes our inner life necessities for prayer, meditation, and Scripture study, essentials that when neglected starve the soul.

Martin includes an observation at the conclusion of each thoughtful reflection. On one entitled *Rest* he makes this observation[16]: "One of the first things I look at when I begin spiritual direction with a pastor is his or her daily planner… If you're working more than 50 hours a week, you're not doing it for God no matter how eloquent your rationalizations… Cut some big chunks out of each week for family, rest, meditation, prayer, and flower sniffing. When you've done that we'll talk more about the path to God."

This thoughtful advice contradicts what one of my District Superintendents told members of our Staff-Parish Relations Committee. In my annual report, I had noted that I was working about sixty-five hours per week. This, at a time when my two youngest children were still at home. The District Superintendent's comment: "He should probably put in ten more hours per week to get the job done." Whew! I think I'm grateful for people like Bill Martin who put life, even life in ministry, in proper perspective.

Take Time to Be Holy

Take time to be holy, speak oft with thy Lord;
abide in him always, and feed on his word.
Make friends of God's children, help those who are weak,
forgetting in nothing his blessing to seek.

WORDS: William D. Longstaff, ca. 1882 (1 Pet. 1:16)

37

The Birthday Party

EVERY ONCE IN A WHILE, if we're open to the Spirit's leading, an inspiration to do something good for another occurs. I say, every once in a while, because most of the time we're so absorbed with our own agendas and concerns in life that we miss God-given opportunities for blessing others. On one occasion Jesus admonished his disciples saying, "... Do you still not perceive or understand? Are your hearts hardened? Do you have eyes, and fail to see? Do you have ears, and fail to hear?" (Mark 8:17-18). I suspect we're like the disciples more often than not.

Nevertheless, there are those times when eyes are opened, and we see clearly, and ears hear distinctly what is being said. It happened to me... This way.

Every other Friday morning I volunteer to drive a van for Neighbors Who Care. I pick up clients, usually six persons making a full load, and take them to a local supermarket to do their weekly grocery shopping. The amount of time it takes to complete the trip, starting at about eight-thirty in the morning, is about four hours. After picking up and delivering the clients to the supermarket, I will get a cup of coffee at the in-store Starbucks and read from my Kindle. Then, as each one finishes his or her shopping, I will load their groceries in the back of the van, escort them up the ramp into the vehicle, and return them to their homes.

On one such occasion, Helen had completed her shopping before the others and was first back to the van. After making sure her seat belt was fastened, she said to me, "You know, Jim, last week was my birthday."

"No," I replied. "I didn't know that. How old are you now?"

She responded somewhat shyly, "I'm ninety-five."

"Wow," I exclaimed. "That's great. Congratulations!"

Soon, others completed their shopping, and I was busy loading the van with their groceries. After I delivered everyone home safely and returned to the office of Neighbors Who Care, it was then that I heard the prompting of the Spirit. "Why don't you do something special for Helen? Why not have a belated birthday party?" *Of course, why not?* I thought.

The following Monday, I returned to the supermarket and talked with someone in Customer Service. I explained that Helen was a faithful customer, and the next time I drove the NWC van, in about two weeks, I wanted to have a surprise birthday party for her in the store. Not only did the representative from the supermarket think it was a fantastic idea, but she also offered a twenty-five dollar credit toward the party—cake, ice cream, punch, plates, napkins, and forks—everything would be complimentary from the store! I was astounded at this display of generosity.

Before the next Friday that I would be driving the van, I called each of the clients and told them of the plan for Helen's surprise birthday party. They were excited and pleased to be in on the plot. The idea was for everyone to gather in the Starbucks customer area instead of starting their shopping. My wife Martha accompanied me this particular morning and was prepared to serve as hostess. The tables had already been set by the store with placemats, plastic utensils, cups, napkins, and balloons! Helen was indeed surprised and quite pleased with the attention.

We all, including some other customers who knew Helen, had a wonderful celebration of her ninety-fifth birthday, belated though it was. It was fun to see the thrill and excitement on the faces of those participating. Photos were taken by Martha on her Kindle device, and the Executive Director of NWC published the story of Helen's birthday party in the next issue of its newsletter.

Thank you, Holy Spirit of God, for the reminder that one of the best feelings in life is when we look and listen around us and discover ways to celebrate and honor the life of someone else.

Spirit of God, Descend upon My Heart

Spirit of God, descend upon my heart;
wean it from earth; through all its pulses move;
stoop to my weakness, mighty as thou art,
and make me love thee as I ought to love.

WORDS: George Croly, 1867 (Gal. 5:25)

❦ 38 ❧

Farewell (a sermon)

ON JUNE 6, 2004, I RETIRED following thirty-five years of full-time service as an ordained minister in The United Methodist Church. The following is the sermon I preached at Willowbrook UMC in Sun City, Arizona. I used, as my texts from Scripture, Philippians 1:3-11 and John 13:2b-9:

"An old story among preachers is the one about a Bishop who had repeatedly sent ministers to a frontier town, and the congregation had repeatedly chased the preachers out of town. In despair, the Bishop sent a youthful, inexperienced man, fresh out of seminary. The young clergyman stayed in that place for several years, and the people seemed content. Finally, the Bishop visited the community and asked the people why they liked the greenhorn minister when they had chased away more competent and experienced clergymen.

"An old-timer replied, 'Well, Bishop, it's this way! We really don't want *no* preacher around here. And this last one you sent comes closest to being that.'

"I share this story on this day when I end a six-year ministry among you. And I wonder, 'Is that why I have lasted *this* long?' Whatever the reason, as I worship with you in this sanctuary which has been our spiritual home these last several years and deliver my final sermon as your senior pastor, I discover the truth again that it's hard to come to the end of any important thing gracefully. Whether it's a letter, a good book, a relationship, a celebration or a life, the final moment is always a difficult one.

"It's easy to understand why this is so. We never get said all that ought to be told or done all that we wanted to do, and the sense of incompleteness about our efforts presses in upon us when the ending is in sight. Memories gather around the threshold of our awareness, and the prospect of closing a chapter we will not read in the same way again, of leaving behind what has been so beautiful, rich and blessed, suggests anything but a casual, indifferent or shallow handling of the departure.

"But as one of my pastor friends once told me, 'Life's second most important lesson is learning to say 'good-bye,' because life is always in the process of change.' We still must move from the familiar to the unfamiliar, from the known to the unknown, from well-worn trails to strange new paths. More than we want to accept, our days that we are privileged to live are made up of transitions, upheavals, changes, and farewells. While life is only understood backward, as someone has suggested, it must always be lived forward. In that awareness, we face this parting, which for Martha and me is very emotional and heartrending, as I know it is for some of you.

"Jesus tried to help the disciples with this truth, talking at length with them to prepare them for his departure from them, as is evident in John's Gospel in what we call 'The Farewell Discourses,' which follow this morning's reading from the Gospel immediately, in chapters 14-16. First, Jesus acts out for the disciples what he wants them to claim as their life of servanthood in love. He girds his waist with a towel and kneels before them as a servant to wash their feet. Then he talks intimately and earnestly with them about how he must leave them, ending the relationship they had grown accustomed to sharing with him so that they can claim a dynamic new relationship with him. It's easy to identify with the disciples' response as they try to cling to Jesus, to seek assurance about what his going away will mean for them and to resist having anything change at all! But because life's second greatest lesson is learning to say 'good-bye,' the disciples had to accept a changed relationship with Jesus, whether they wanted to or not.

"Then the Apostle Paul's words in his letter to his friends at Philippi read like a farewell letter. In it Paul thanks the people of Philippi for their many years of constancy, support, affirmation and caring concern, saying, 'I thank my God in all my remembrance of you, always in every prayer of mine for you all, making my prayer with joy, thankful for your partnership in the Gospel from the first day until now … It is right for me to feel thus about you all, because I hold you in my heart, *for you are all partakers with me of grace.'* (What a beautiful phrase—'partakers with me of grace.')

"But then further on in the letter, Paul encourages them:

> *Only let your manner of life be worthy of the Gospel of Christ, so that whether I (even) come to see you (in person) or am absent from you, I may hear of you that you stand firm in one spirit, with one mind striving side by side for the faith of the gospel.*

And bringing his letter to a close, he utters those memorable lines:

> *Rejoice in the Lord always, again I say Rejoice! ... Finally friends, whatever is true, whatever is honorable, whatever is just, whatever is pure, whatever is lovely, whatever is gracious, if there is any excellence, if there is anything worthy of praise, think about these things. What you have learned and received and heard and seen in me, do; and the God of peace will be with you.*

Yes, life's second most important lesson is to learn to say 'good-bye!' to what has been.

"But Jesus and Paul also make clear that life's first most important lesson is to live out God's love and move forward with faith to embrace the new, to let our lives be worthy of the Gospel of Christ, to live a servant life in a world that cries out to us to stop, to kneel down to help and to stay as long as our being there meets human need, to embody unconditional love in who we are, what we do, what we say and what we value. God created us so that we need each other, and shaped life so that its most significant meaning is found in relationships of sharing, constancy and trust, of reaching out to others and letting them come close to us.

"Wayne Oates, in his book *Pastoral Counseling*, recounts what a 27-year-old woman said to a pastoral counselor during her *first* visit[17]:

> *I have lived ever since I became a Christian on the assumption that with only God's help and my efforts combined could I*

face life successfully. Now that has collapsed. God and I cannot live alone. We both need other people.

"Yes! We need other people to receive God's grace, and God needs other people through whom God offers God's grace.

"Hasn't that been your experience? It has indeed been mine over the past thirty-five years of ordained ministry and even the years of ministry as a student pastor and as a member of the laity before that. I look across those years and am keenly aware of how God's grace appeared for me in the people who entered my life—some to whom I ministered but most who ministered to me. In their gestures of love, in the truth they were for me, in their kindness, concern and affirmation, in their sense of humor and perspective, in the beauty they created, in the faith that centered them, God's grace came alive for me. Jesus drew near and stood among us and joy-filled what were holy moments.

"We do need each other in love. To be partakers together of grace is to labor side by side in the Gospel together—indeed, to be the Gospel for each other, to live out the good news that God is at work in us, giving us each other, giving us faith in Christ, giving us joy and sending us out together to heal a broken world.

"In one of his books, Henri Nouwen tells how it happened for him with one of his former students. He writes:[18]

> *I vividly remember the day on which a former student came back to school and entered my office with the disarming remark: "I have no problem this time, no question to ask you. I do not need your counselor advice, but I simply want to celebrate some time with you." We went outside and sat on the lawn, facing each other and talked a little about what life had been for us the last year, about our work, our common friends, and about the restlessness of our hearts. Then slowly as the minutes passed by we became silent. Not an embarrassing silence, but a silence that could bring us closer together than the many small and big events of the last year. We would hear a few cars passing and the noise of someone who was emptying a trash can somewhere. But that*

> *did not interfere. The silence which grew between us was warm, gentle and vibrant. Once in a while, we looked at each other with the beginning of a smile pushing away the last remnants of fear and wariness. It seemed that while the silence grew deeper around us, we became more and more aware of God's presence embracing both of us. Then he said to me, "It's good to be here." And I replied, "Yes, it's good to be together again," and after that, we were silent again for a long period. And as a peace filled the space between us, he said hesitantly, "When I look at you it is as if I am in the presence of Christ." I did not feel surprised nor did I protest but only answered, "It is the Christ in you who recognizes the Christ in me." "Yes," he said, "He indeed is in our midst." Then he spoke words which entered into my soul as the most healing words I had ever heard: "From now on, wherever you go, or wherever I go, all the ground between us will be holy ground."*

"I want to say that similar moments have occurred for us with you—moments which were infused with the presence of Christ. Moments of silence and laughter, moments of silence and the anguish of suffering, moments of silence and the sounds of grief, moments of silence and spirited conversation, moments of silence and the beautiful sounds of deeds of love being shared.

"And that's why 'from now on, wherever you go, or wherever we go, all the ground between us will be holy ground,' because we are 'partakers together of grace.'

"And that's why we dare to live forward, ready to embrace all that shall be. In that spirit, I prayerfully hope you greet your new senior pastor as he comes to serve here among you with his wife as a 'partaker with you of grace.' The greatest testimonies you can give to my ministry among you is to welcome them both, want the best for them, support them, pray for them, and go forward with them on your journey of faith, with a daring vision of the Kingdom of God made real in certain deeds of love.

"After June 30, that's the official date, I will no longer be your senior pastor, and I hope you understand that's why I will not return here for weddings or memorial services or other occasions that call for a pastoral presence or function. This is because I will not rob my successor of his rightful opportunity to be your pastor, to walk with you in joy and stand with you in the shadows or pray with you at the border moments of life.

"But I will always be your friend in Christ, *we* will always be your friends in Christ because in the years we were privileged to spend together and in the years to come, we are always partakers together of grace. 'From now on, wherever you go, or wherever we go, all the ground between us will be holy ground.'

"The words of Tim Hansel are unique to Martha and me, and with them, I will close:[19] 'There isn't much that I can do, but I can share my friendship with you, and I can share my life with you, and I can share my Lord with you and often a prayer or two—as on our way we go.'

"As Martha and I go on our way to retirement and part-time work at the church in Sun Lakes, we're very grateful for you and thank God for you! You can be sure that we will remember you and our year's together. God bless all of you—each one of you—with the power of the Risen Christ! Amen!"

Blest Be the Tie That Binds

Blest be the tie that binds our hearts in Christian love;
the fellowship of kindred minds is like to that above.
When we asunder part, it gives us inward pain;
but we shall still be joined in heart, and hope to meet again.

WORDS: John Fawcett, 1782

39

On Writing

AFTER I PUBLISHED MY MEMOIR and started offering and selling it to friends in the churches I had served, I received a variety of responses and feedback. "You and I had similar childhood experiences." "Boy, I sure grew up different from you." "How do you remember so much detail of your life's encounters?" "Man, you have had a fascinating life!" "I had to laugh as the same thing happened to me!" But the comment I heard often, and one that I took as a compliment was, "Jim, you write just like you preach. I can hear your voice in every story!"

A recent line from a movie caught my attention. The wife of a would-be writer asked him, "Why are you so driven to write?" His response was intriguing: "I guess it's a way of keeping things alive. You know, saving things that will eventually die. If I write it down, then it'll last forever."

I guess that's part of why I have been writing stories from my life. I didn't know much about the lives of my great-grandparents, much less my grandparents. A cousin helped my grandmother write several experiences from her life, and I heard several oral stories about my parents and uncles and aunts. But these were the kinds of memorable and funny things that were often repeated. I want something in print for my grandchildren and great-granddaughters to remember about me, but I'm not so naïve as to think it'll last forever.

I digress. There's no trick to my writing technique. I write as if I were having a conversation with someone, like telling a humorous joke or something interesting that happened to me. My vocabulary is adequate, but I don't make a practice of using big words that most people would never use in casual conversation. I like the backdoor insult William Faulkner wrote concerning another writer, Ernest Hemingway. Faulkner said, "He (Hemingway) has never been known to use a word that might send a reader to the dictionary." That could be said of me, Mr. Faulkner. Moreover, it's annoying to me to hear a preacher show off his or her education by using Greek or Hebrew words in a sermon. I especially dislike the exaggerated pronunciation of such words as "Gawd" or "Lawd" in public prayers. Yuk!

Furthermore, it's irritating to me to hear a preacher say, "I'm probably going to butcher the pronunciation of this word, but …" For crying out loud, use the dictionary and look up the pronunciation and practice saying it (even phonetically writing it in the sermon notes) before delivering the sermon! This failure to do so smacks of laziness.

My most significant difficulty in writing is with punctuation. When I finished writing my memoir, I asked several friends to help with this area. To my astonishment, everyone had a different take on the rules of punctuation. As did my publisher. Eventually, I have come to rely on an online English writing-enhancement platform developed by Grammarly, Inc., headquartered in San Francisco, and launched in 2009. Though not entirely without its flaws, this checker eliminates most grammatical errors, referring to 250 grammar rules, and surveys each paragraph as it is being written. This useful computer tool was discovered by my wife Martha as she wrote her book, *Out of My Mind.* I only wish I had found this program before spending hundreds of dollars for proofreading by my publishers who, it seemed, merely used Word for Windows spelling and grammar check.

When I was in high school, I had a knowledgeable teacher for a class in Physics. However, he would discover who the smart students were, the ones who quickly grasped the concepts he was teaching, and brought them along at his pace of learning. Unfortunately, the other students like me got left behind. I remember this frustrating experience to this day and try to avoid this when writing or preaching. An old preacher used to tell me, "Make sure everyone's aboard the train before leaving the station." You bet I will!

James D. Wood

Tell Me the Stories of Jesus

Tell me the stories of Jesus I love to hear;
things I would ask him to tell me if he were here:
scenes by the wayside, tales of the sea,
stories of Jesus, tell them to me.

WORDS: William H. Parker, 1885 (Mt. 19:13-
15; 21:8-9; Mk. 10:13-16; 11:8-10; Jn. 12:13)

40

Rocky

MOST PERSONS WITH THE NAME "ROCKY," are those associated with the world of sports, namely those in professional boxing. There is Rocky Marciano, one-time World Heavyweight Champion. Another is Rocky Graziano, who held the World Middleweight title. Of course, there is also the fictional Rocky Balboa played by the actor Sylvester Stallone.

Others include Rocky Colavito, baseball; Rocky Bleier, football; Rocky Carroll, television actor on NCIS; and Rocky Lynch, pop singer. Oh, and don't forget the wonderfully creative, animated TV show, "Rocky and Bullwinkle."

So what's my interest with the name Rocky? Well, it has to do with a little girl who lived across the street from us during my childhood in Pacific Beach. She was a couple of years younger than me, and her parents and my parents were friends socially. Her father and mine worked at Consolidated Aircraft during World War II. Our families attended the same church; I found out later. Her name was Jo-Raquel Tejada, and she was skinny, had black hair in braided pigtails and, if memory serves me, always seemed to have a runny nose. Her family moved out of The Projects before we did and she attended La Jolla High School, a school I would have attended if we had not moved to another community during my junior high years.

Raquel grew up to be a beautiful young woman and married her high school sweetheart, Jim Welch. You guessed it—I'm talking about Raquel Welch, who took on the nickname "Rocky," hence the title of this story.

Recently a bowling friend, knowing of my childhood association with Raquel, gave me a mini-biography written by her. She entitled the book,

Raquel: Beyond the Cleavage. Though much of its content deals with some personal struggles, her involvement with Hollywood, the celebrities she has known, her husbands and children, women's health and beauty tips, and how she sees herself as a woman, it was the last chapter that caught my interest, "The Spiritual Woman."[20]

In this chapter, Raquel describes how, in the past ten years of her life, she reconnected with God and sought out a community of faith to nurture this shift of direction. Her thoughts began to focus on finding spiritual answers following the death of her mother and the successful surgery of her sister for ovarian cancer.

It had been more than fifty years since she attended church. So Raquel prayed to the God of her childhood and discovered that God was still there. Thus, her spiritual journey resumed.

She found a modest, unassuming church, one that was cheerful and friendly. The people welcomed Raquel, and she felt comfortable sitting among these parishioners who had not a superficial bone in their bodies. She became a member of this church, and its people became her brothers and sisters in faith.

Raquel concludes by writing, "Together we form a fellowship where I can reaffirm my beliefs and worship every Sunday. When I'm in their midst, I'm just Raquel, not anybody special." To which I would add, "Yes, you are somebody special. And so are you, dear reader. You're a child of God, precious and beloved, worthy of the one who died for you, the one who enables this right relationship with God and gives us hope! I would encourage you to go out and boldly claim that incredible legacy and inheritance!"

O Love That Wilt Not Let Me Go

O Love that wilt not let me go, I rest my weary soul in thee;
I give thee back the life I owe, that in thine ocean depths its flow
may richer, fuller be.

WORDS: George Matheson, 1882

41

Thirty Year Celebration (a sermon)

IN THE YEAR 2017, THE UNITED METHODIST CHURCH in Sun Lakes, the church of our retirement, celebrated its thirtieth birthday or anniversary. The pastors and a group on the planning committee worked hard to ensure a celebration that would be meaningful and remembered.

A quilt was crafted depicting scenes of our church's ministry and mission as well as some events, such as the 9-11 tragedy, that occurred during the church's lifetime. Our conference's bishop, Robert Hoshibata, was invited to preach the Sunday the anniversary was to be featured. Our music director, Cris Evans, composed a rousing anthem for the worship service. A dinner that evening was to be held at one of the country clubs in Sun Lakes and over three hundred persons would be attending. A former associate pastor, popular with many in the congregation, was scheduled to speak. It seemed that everything had been planned down to the smallest detail.

However, no matter how carefully a project is planned, something may still go wrong with it. I'm reminded of a saying adapted from a line in "To a Mouse," by Robert Burns: "The best-laid schemes o' Mice an' Men / Gang aft agley (oft go astray or awry)."

One month (seemed shorter than that) before the big event, I received a phone call from the senior pastor. It appeared that the scheduled dinner speaker was experiencing some health problems and wouldn't be able to attend. He asked if I would be willing to fill in as the speaker. After a brief moment of hesitation, I agreed. I could hear him give a sigh of relief.

I was able to adapt my message for the special dinner occasion from a sermon that I had once preached. For those who were unable to attend the dinner (or who have short memories), I have included the talk in this story. It is as follows:

"The Source of Our Strength"
Hebrews 12:1-2

In one of Max Lucado's books, he tells of a woman who went up a mountain she should have avoided. It's a humorous story and suffice it to say, Lucado declares, "There are certain mountains we were never made to climb. Ascend them, and you'll end up bruised and embarrassed. Stay away from them, and you'll sidestep a lot of stress."[21]

Well, that may be. Nevertheless, there are times when God asks us to climb mountains, and for the past thirty years our church has responded to God's challenge to climb mountains—mountains in keeping with God's vision of our being a courageous church, loving like Jesus, acting for justice, and united in hope. It hasn't always been an easy task. The world, our country, state, and community have all seen attempts to find ways to incorporate God's vision into our ministry and mission when we've ended up bruised and experienced a lot of stress, but we've ever been embarrassed.

The writer of Hebrews knew about this difficulty. The letter is addressed to Christians who were facing a frightening and uncertain future. It's sometime around the year 100 A.D., so these people represent the third and fourth generations of Christians. They can recall the faith of their grandparents who had eagerly expected the return of Jesus. And, as the writer of Hebrews reminds them, there was a time when their own faith was strong, and they had stood up to threats and public torment. But now that robust and sure confidence was slipping away. Christ had not returned as anticipated. Persecution was increasing. The future looked grim. The initial enthusiasm of faith was declining, and the community was unraveling. What in the world would give those Christians the strength and courage to move boldly into the future?

The writer of Hebrews tells them: Christ has gone first. Christ is already leading the way:

> *Let us run with perseverance the race that is set before us, looking to Jesus the pioneer and perfecter of our faith, who for the sake of the joy that was set before him endured the cross, disregarding its shame, and has taken his seat at the right hand of the throne of God.*

Christ has gone first. Christ is in front of us beckoning us on. I saw this encouragement played out when my grandchildren were younger. They had come to visit us one summer, and we took them to the children's swimming pool at Oakwood. I watched a mother already in the water and her little girl in a life jacket on the deck of the pool trying to jump in. The child would approach the pool very slowly. Tiny steps. She got right to the edge. And she started squatting down as if to spring up over the water. But instead, she stood back up and grimaced. Her whole body said, "Do I want to do this or not?" Again and again, she would get poised to jump, then stand up and stare suspiciously at the water. But all the while her mother was in the pool right in front of her. Her mother started reaching out her arms. She was saying: "Come on, Honey. I'm right here. You'll be fine." And finally, the little girl sprang up into the air and came down into the pool with a splash. Her mother caught her, and the two of them laughed with delight.

I think many of us relive the pattern of that little girl when we face what is unfamiliar and fearful. Perhaps a new stage of life, a new location, a world that no longer runs like the world we grew up in, an unforeseen challenge to live our faith, to carry on the ministry of Christ in places and ways that unnerve us. At such times it's helpful to remember that Christ has gone first. Christ is like that mother. Christ is standing ready to catch us and calling to us: "Come on. Don't be afraid. Plunge in. I've gone first. I'm right here. You'll be fine."

As if it were not enough that Christ has gone first, the writer of Hebrews reminds us of generation after generation of real heroes and heroines in Hebrew Scripture, those who preceded Christ. Chapter 11 is the prelude to the verses we have read. It's a litany of women and men who "by faith" endured every form of suffering and pain and disillusionment. The author gathers them all together in a dramatic image calling them a cloud of witnesses. This cloud, not to be confused with computer data storage facilities, includes those who have gone before us here in this congregation. This cloud surrounds us this day, ready to cheer us on as if we were about to begin a long-distance race in a huge athletic stadium. We can hear them cheering, in the roar of their encouragement. Think of them now… Say their names quietly in your hearts and minds… Give thanks to God for their lives and the influence of love they had and continued to have on your life.

The writer of Hebrews is there too, calling out "lay aside every weight and the sin that clings so closely to us." For a moment, our hearts grow faint. We think we don't have what it takes, but then the crowd begins a great chant: "Run the race, run the race! Look to Jesus, look to Jesus!"

I can think of times when I've heard them, loud and distinct. People in our home church. Members of the nine churches I've served, including this one. Bishop Hoshibata, in his message this morning, mentioned a son whose path in life was difficult. I can relate because we have a daughter, a prodigal daughter, who took a similar path. During a time of great turmoil, disappointment, and sadness in our lives, Martha held me close as I sobbed and I heard them through her comforting presence: "Run the race, run the race! Look to Jesus, look to Jesus!"

There was the time when, during my last year of college, Martin Luther King, Jr. was murdered, assassinated. An African-American friend invited Martha and me to his church a week or so afterward. And I remember the people of his congregation, suspicious and wary of us at first, soon warming up to us and making us feel most welcome. They had been through the wars of discrimination and bigotry, people who stood against all that was working to destroy their children and their neighborhoods. When they rose in worship to pray, to preach, to sing, I could hear the whole cloud of heaven's witnesses singing: "Run the race, run the race! Look to Jesus, look to Jesus!"

There have been countless times in worship when I've climbed into the pulpit bearing with me the burdens that are common to the humanity of us all. Later, as I was sharing the bread and cup and listening to the choir, I heard deeper notes in the music they were singing, and it was the music of the cloud of witnesses: "Run the race, run the race! Look to Jesus, look to Jesus!"

Those are some of the times when I have heard the great cloud of witnesses. I could share other times. When have you listened to the cloud? Think now: When have you heard those witnesses, calling to you, "Run the race, run the race! Look to Jesus, look to Jesus!" Perhaps you heard them and didn't realize it. Maybe it was a surge of hope in your heart when things looked hopeless. Perhaps it was a friend's encouragement. Maybe it was a moment of silent prayer so still that it was filled with a mysterious sense of presence, the presence of God's Holy Spirit. Perhaps it was a time when you stood against injustice, and your knees were shaking, and your voice is quivering, but you heard a voice crying out within for what is right and good and just.

Or perhaps you've been running for a stretch without the sound of the cloud of witnesses in your heart. Then listen this week with renewed attentiveness for their voices of encouragement. For when you hear them, you will see that Christ has gone first and you will receive strength to follow him.

I remind you of the words of the anthem the choir sang last week: "Until the race is run, until the journey's done, until the crown is won ... Lord, teach me your way." We are not alone. Continue the race and look to Jesus.

I'll close with a story that ran several years ago in the newspaper, one I shared at our 20th-anniversary celebration. You may remember it. The story showed a photo of a woman leaning over and listening to a man's chest. The caption under the picture read, "Woman listens to the heartbeat of her only son." The accompanying article talked about how the woman's son was killed in a tragic automobile accident, but through the miracle of organ donation, some of his organs were able to be harvested and passed on to others needing transplants. In this case, she was literally listening to her son's heartbeat as its rhythmic beat gave life to someone else.

I wonder... If God were to put his ear to our own chest, would God hear the heartbeat of his only Son? Would God hear the pulse of his only Son, whose heart was broken so that ours might be mended? I pray that through our attempts to integrate God's vision of ministry and mission, others in our community may hear the rhythmic beat of God's heart—a heart that continues to pulsate with love and grace in this place called Sun Lakes United Methodist Church. Amen!

We've a Story to Tell to the Nations

We've a story to tell to the nations,
that shall turn their hearts to the right,
a story of truth and mercy, a story of peace and light,
a story of peace and light.
For the darkness shall turn to dawning,
and the dawning to noonday bright;
and Christ's great kingdom shall come on earth,
the kingdom of love and light.

WORDS: H. Ernest Nichol, 1896

✂ 42 ✂

All in the Family

OVER THE YEARS OF MY MINISTRY, almost fifty years now, I have probably conducted hundreds of weddings, baptisms, and funerals or memorial services. Some marriages have been in outdoor settings, homes, and a couple in other countries (Mexico and England). Some funerals or graveside services have taken place in mortuaries or cemeteries. I conducted one in England in 2002 during a church exchange. Except for one home baptism, most have taken place within the worship service on Sunday mornings in the churches I served. I have always considered it an honor and privilege to officiate at these crucial milestones in the lives of the persons involved.

I have been uniquely privileged to be asked to conduct these services for members of my family. I have married our daughters and our son. I officiated at the wedding of Martha's youngest sister and her husband on Thanksgiving Day. I was able to marry Martha's mother and her fourth husband in the chapel of their church in National City, California. I married my brother's oldest daughter in Mexico and our oldest granddaughter in 2017. I am hoping to marry our other granddaughter in the fall of 2019, though this still hasn't been confirmed. Unfortunately, some of these marriages did not last. I regret, especially, that I turned down the offers to conduct the second marriages of our youngest daughter and son. I feel sad that I put something else before my love for them.

Baptisms, like weddings, are always a joyful occasion. Family members that I have baptized have all, with one exception, been infants. When our oldest daughter was born, I was not an ordained minister. The pastor in our church at that time did not observe infant baptism. Instead, he emphasized infant dedication to the Lord. Years later, after being ordained and appointed to my first church beyond seminary, I baptized her following her confirmation. Our son was born during a time when the pastor mentioned above was sent to another congregation. Our new pastor observed infant baptism, and we had him baptized then. He is the only child I did not baptize myself.

I baptized our youngest daughter shortly after we adopted her during my seminary years. Also, I was privileged to baptize my brother's daughters. Then, as our seven grandchildren came along their parents brought them forward for the Sacrament of Holy Baptism. More recently, in September 2017, I was privileged to baptize our first great-granddaughter. Two other great-granddaughters have entered the world since that year. What happy, joyous occasions all these births have been!

The reader may have noticed above that I made a distinction between a funeral and a memorial service. A funeral is a service held to memorialize a deceased person with their body present. A memorial is a service conducted to memorialize a person with their body not present. However, if a burial occurs before the service for a loved one, the service is considered a memorial service. Most of these services for the family have been memorial services. The first one I conducted was for a great aunt on my mother's side of the family. I officiated at the graveside services for an uncle and aunt (my mother's sister and her husband) at different times. Also, their son-in-law who was accidentally killed. Finally, Martha's mother, again in her church in National City, California.

As I have gotten older, I will attain (if that's the proper word) the age of eighty this November of 2018, I have turned down requests from various church members to officiate at, primarily, their funerals or memorial services. I say primarily because our retirement church in Sun Lakes, Arizona, is composed mainly of older persons. There is not much call for weddings or baptisms.

Moreover, I believe firmly that these are occasions for the full-time pastors to have their relationships with the congregation strengthened. I would encourage this bonding and deepening level of trust and love between pastor and parishioner.

I still teach some Bible classes (though I can see an end to these) and preach once in a great while, but these opportunities offer some advance time for planning and preparation. Funerals and memorial services usually don't give much time for this, and I'm just not able to cope with the stress involved, at least not as I was when younger. I know that I've disappointed some by saying, "No" to their requests, but most have understood my feelings. Thank you for your gracious understanding. Blessings!

Happy the Home When God Is There
Happy the home when God is there,
and love fills every breast, when one their wish,
and one their prayer, and one their heavenly rest.

WORDS: Henry Ware, Jr., 1846

43

The Folly of Preaching

THE TITLE OF THIS PARTICULAR STORY comes from one of Paul's letters to the church at Corinth in which he vigorously defends both the message of the gospel and his own manner of proclaiming it:

> *For the message about the cross is foolishness to those who are perishing, but to us who are being saved it is the power of God... Has not God made foolish the wisdom of the world? For since, in the wisdom of God, the world did not know God through wisdom, God decided through the foolishness of our proclamation [preaching] to save those who believe. (1 Corinthians 1:19.)*

Is preaching really foolishness? It obviously is in some sense because Paul uses that word. Indeed, preachers will often say that there are times when they feel foolish as they try to bring a word from God to those living in the midst of secular culture. I confess that I have felt this way on several occasions.

I recall a time when I had started back to college after having experienced God's call to ordained ministry when another seminary-bound student from our church called me on a Sunday afternoon. He was in his last year at the university I would soon be attending. He explained that he was taking a course in communications and wanted to interview me at my home. When I asked the purpose of the interview, he stated that he would tell me after our conversation. I agreed to meet with him the following day.

The next day came, and my friend arrived promptly at my home at our agreed upon time. He set up a tape recorder and with a microphone in hand, turned it on and asked me this question: "Jim, what do you recall about yesterday's sermon?"

I blinked and then thoughtfully said, "Well, I remember the introduction and the first point of the sermon. I remember two of the illustrations but can't recall the second or third point. I do remember the conclusion and its accompanying illustration." Then I proceeded to relate my recollection of what I had heard.

When I finished, my friend turned off the tape recorder and said, "You did very well. You're the fifth person I've interviewed from our church, and you're only one who remembered anything that was said in yesterday's sermon." He went on to say that the results were typical of people trying to remember what was said in any oral proclamation or speech. I was astonished. Was this the meaning of the phrase, "the folly of preaching"?

To be sure, when Paul preached in Athens, his hearers laughed because his message seemed foolish. When the early ambassadors of the gospel came to the Greeks, proclaiming that the indescribable God had become a man in human flesh to die for our salvation that contradicted everything they knew about philosophy. The fundamental principle of Greek philosophy was that the mind was separate from matter, that spirit was separate from the flesh. It was inconceivable to the Greek that there could be an incarnation. What appeared to be the height of folly is, according to Paul, actually the wisdom of God.

Nevertheless, what about the people sitting in worship Sunday after Sunday? What do they regard when they hear the words coming from the pulpit? I suppose in the minds of many, the content of preaching, and perhaps even the delivery of the sermon itself seems a very foolish thing. Unless their hearts are receptive to the Holy Spirit of God. Unless there is a deep hunger for comfort in the time of grieving the loss of a loved one. Unless life's circumstances and evil's influences are overwhelming and they're searching for God's strengthening and loving presence. Unless their life is mired in an endless round of meaningless and they're wondering if there is something else, something with purpose. Unless they come to worship seeking hope and assurance of a Savior who proclaims he will never leave us and that we are never alone. Then it is that folly is transformed into faith, and faith proclaims a certainty beyond all empirical evidence.

I know because it happened to me at a pivotal point in my life. I could have ignored a prodding from God to follow a sometimes harsh and challenging path. It would have been easy to give in to my fears and reluctance. Instead, in a time of wrestling and agonizing over whether to take this new path that was put before me, I opened my spirit to God's leading through prayer, Scripture, devotional books, and, yes, words from the pulpit. Then, as fears dissolved and newfound confidence and assurance emerged from within, I realized a truth from Jesus' explanation of his parables, "But blessed are your eyes, for they see, and your ears, for they hear. Truly I tell you, many prophets and righteous people longed to see what you see, but did not see it, and to hear what you hear, but did not hear it." (Matthew 13:16-17).

Through the folly of preaching, among other means considered foolishness by unbelievers, I received new eyes, new ears, a new heart, and a new purpose in life. Thanks be to God!

Spirit of God, Descend upon My Heart
Teach me to love thee as thine angels love,
one holy passion filling all my frame;
the kindling of the heaven descended Dove,
my heart an altar, and thy love the flame.

WORDS: George Croly, 1867 (Gal. 5:25)

44

The Voice

AT FIRST GLANCE, THE ABOVE TITLE may bring to mind the four-time Emmy Award-winning television show "The Voice." It features the most talented vocalists from across the United States invited to compete in the blockbuster vocal competition each season. That's not what comes to my mind, but allow me to enlighten.

I recently heard a sermon by one of our church's six retired pastors (I'm one among them). His preaching focused on Psalm 23 and John 10. The Hebrew Bible's passage lifted up the image of God as the Divine Shepherd, while the Gospel passage dealt with Jesus as the Good Shepherd. It was a marvelous sermon and touched me in several ways.

One of the ways my heart was warmed was in recalling some words that I had read in Adam Hamilton's book. It was the chapter on "The Holy Spirit" where Hamilton discusses the voices that influence and shape us. He writes, "We all have voices we hear in our heads or deep down in our heart—some good voices, some not so good."[22]

This thought, coupled with the passage in John's Gospel, brought to mind the question of what voices do I listen? Do I listen to family, friends, media, politicians, business leaders, colleagues? How are the voices to which I listen shaping my soul? Are these voices leading me to become more like the person God wants me to be, or less?

Hamilton continues, "The Holy Spirit, or the Spirit of God, is God's way of leading us, guiding us, forming and shaping us; of God's power and presence to comfort and encourage us and to make us the people God wants us to be. The Spirit is the voice of God whispering, wooing,

147

and beckoning us. And in listening to this voice and being shaped by this power, we find that we become most fully and authentically human."[23]

The voice I want to listen to and give my utmost attention and devotion is the Great Shepherd described by John in his Gospel. Take a look at what John declares:

> *The one who enters by the gate is the shepherd of the sheep. The gatekeeper opens the gate for him, and the sheep hear his voice. He calls his own sheep by name and leads them out. When he has brought out all his own, he goes ahead of them, and the sheep follow him because they know his voice. (John 10:2-4.)*

The Great Deceiver, the personification of evil who has many forms, continues to whisper in our ears, daily for most of us, beckoning us to do the very things that will bring harm to others and ourselves. Ignoring this beguiling voice is difficult. When I ignore the voice of the Good Shepherd, I am less than the person God desires me to be.

In my memoir, *This Is My Story, This Is My Song*, I briefly described the way I saw myself as a minister of the gospel. In some churches, regardless of the particular denomination, and in some congregations, the pastor is sometimes referred to as "the shepherd leading the flock." When we visited Ireland several years ago, we saw how a working shepherd guided his flock of sheep. He used a very intelligent and obedient Border Collie to help herd his livestock. The shepherd used various whistles as commands. The dog listened to "the voice" of his master and knew what direction to guide the sheep.

That's the way I see myself as a pastor—not as a shepherd leading a flock, but as a sheep dog whose responsibility it is to listen to the commands of the Great Shepherd, maneuvering his flock, his people, gently in the direction the Master requests.

The Voice of God Is Calling

The voice of God is calling its summons in our day;
Isaiah heard in Zion, and we now hear God say:
"Whom shall I send to succor my people in their need?
Whom shall I send to loosen the bonds of shame and greed?"
WORDS: John Haynes Holmes, 1913 (Is. 6:8)

∾ 45 ∾

Einstein

NOT *THE* ALBERT EINSTEIN, a German-born theoretical physicist who developed the theory of relativity, one of the two pillars of modern physics, and whose work is also known for its influence on the philosophy of science. This well-known genius shares the same birthday as my wife, although he was sixty-one years of age when she was born.

No, the Einstein to which I refer is the Einstein Bros. Bagels, an American bagel and coffee chain. Melvin and Elmo are the names of the brothers. I don't know if these are fictitious or real persons, but I know they started their own Facebook page on April 30, 2015. So far they have 129 likes and 11 comments. Interesting, huh? Well, maybe not.

The purpose of this somewhat amusing piece of writing relates to a morning habit that my wife and I have acquired over the past two years. We have been frequenting Einstein Bros. Bagels during this time three or four times per week. That may be one reason we find ourselves dieting to lose weight from time to time. Hey, is that any different from you being addicted to Starbucks? At least Einstein coffee is cheaper. I usually get a refill cup (I supply my own cup from home) of Vanilla Hazelnut coffee (senior discount) for $1.35. Then, I refill my cup again before leaving.

We have become such frequent patrons that many of the employees, including the manager, know and refer to us by name. In fact, one time when the queue of customers was so long it stretched out the door, I approached one of the employees and asked, "Do you have a favorite customer policy here?"

She coyly answered, "Why, yes we do."

I responded, "Would I be on that list?"

Amused, she said, "Why, yes you are."

Encouraged by her reply, I asked if I could place my order with her and pay for it later.

"Of course, you may. I'll have your order out to you right away."

Okay, not surprising to those of you who know me well.

We have also become acquainted with many other regular customers, including members of our church, and enjoy the socializing aspect of this relationship. People we have often seen through our breakfast time at Einstein, have recognized us at doctor appointments and other restaurants in the Sun Lakes and Chandler area. Though we usually read from our Kindle books during this morning meal, we sometimes engage in lively conversation with members of our Einstein family.

I will hasten to say that we don't always get a bagel with cream cheese (Einstein's term is schmear). Our choice includes a variety of items. Sometimes we order a bacon, cheese, and egg sandwich, other times a yogurt parfait. Sometimes a fruit cup, other times a muffin or a banana. Our orders depend on mood and whether or not we're trying to cut down on the calories because of weight gain.

I was somewhat mystified as to the closing words of my hymn for this writing. My humorous mind kicked in as I contemplated several. One hymn's first line was, "All my hope is firmly grounded" (get it? Grounded?). Another was, "And can it be that I should gain." Enough already! Anyway, because of the sacredness of food shared and food provided by others through the grace of God, I settled on the following (words in brackets are those more familiar to me):

Be Present at Our Table, Lord

Be present at our table, Lord;

be here and everywhere adored;

these creatures [mercies] bless, and grant that we

may feast in paradise [fellowship] with thee.

WORDS: John Cennick, 1741

46

Decluttering

I'M A PERSON WHO DOESN'T LIKE CLUTTER. At an early age, my mother taught me to be tidy, neat and orderly. As part of my discipline in early childhood, I learned to make my bed each morning, pick up my dirty clothes and put them in the hamper, hang up my jacket in the closet, conduct my personal hygiene, and make sure my shirttail was tucked in and my shoes were brushed before going to school. This routine practice of avoiding disorder was expected by my parents for all their children.

This routine of personal neatness and of having my room and possessions in an organized arrangement never became an obsession with me. As a child, I played outside most of the time and got dirty and grimy. But when it got too dark to play anymore, I would be called inside to get cleaned up and ready for bed. Strange, now that I think about it, my family during the 1940s only took a bath (I never heard of a shower until junior high) once a week, usually Saturday night. This particular evening of the week brought another aspect of tidiness—it was my responsibility to polish everyone's shoes in preparation for Sunday school and church the next morning.

As an aside, being clean has traditionally been a sign of spiritual purity or goodness, as in "Don't forget to wash your ears—cleanliness is next to godliness." This phrase was first recorded in a sermon by John Wesley in 1778. In it, Wesley indicated that the proverb was already well known in the form with which we are familiar today, but the idea is ancient, found in Babylonian and Hebrew religious tracts. Wrote Wesley: "Slovenliness [there's a word we seldom use anymore] is no part of religion." Nevertheless, it is my understanding that the adage "cleanliness is next to Godliness" is not a quote from the Bible and had nothing to do with piousness.

The habit of being a "neatnik" carried over in later years. It especially paid dividends when I served in the U.S. Navy. I became aware of another saying while completing my obligatory stint with Uncle Sam: "A clean ship is a happy ship!" Oh, yes, indeed it is. The Chief Petty Officers were especially fond of saying this, and more than once I found myself, along with several other recruits, "policing the area," picking up cigarette butts and other miscellaneous debris.

I stated above that I never became obsessive-compulsive as a result of this discipline. At least, not that it occupied my mind in an unhealthy way. Nevertheless, when I went back to school to resume my studies after experiencing God's call to ordained ministry, I discovered that I could not bring myself to accomplish my homework if our home was in disarray—if dishes were in the sink, the carpet needed vacuuming, furniture required dusting, magazines and newspapers weren't neatly arranged and folded. Once I put everything in order, then I could tackle the schoolwork I had been assigned.

All of this is a prelude to the purpose of writing this story. Recently, my wife and I have been engaged in "decluttering" our home. As of this writing, we've been in our home for fourteen years. That's the longest we have lived in any one place ever! We have accumulated a lot of stuff during that time. Should something drastic occur in one or both of our lives, and we are rendered unable to take care of ourselves physically, we would have to depend on loved ones. We don't want the burden of sifting through our possessions to fall on our family. Therefore, we've been taking care of this task now while we're able. Some in our family had to do this inconvenient and tiresome chore for others who passed from this life to the next. Sorry, but that's not the way I was raised. Indeed, "a clean ship is a happy ship."

All Things Bright and Beautiful

All things bright and beautiful, all creatures great and small,
all things wise and wonderful: the Lord God made them all.
God gave us eyes to see them, and lips that we might tell
how great is God Almighty, who has made all things well.
WORDS: Cecil Frances Alexander, 1848 (Gen. 1:31)

47

On Speaking

MANY PEOPLE HAVE A FEAR OF public speaking. As mentioned early on in my memoir, I had this irrational fear. It was only after I finally agreed to God's calling me to ordained ministry that this fear was lifted and I came to enjoy the experience of preaching. It has been over fifty years since that time, and I feel constrained to write about some everyday bad habits that many presenters, even otherwise smart, accomplished professionals seem not to be able to avoid.

Local television news, weather, and sports personalities are among the worst offenders. They are trained to speak rapidly to get as much information as possible in the short time they have allotted. Thus, especially to ears of the elderly, their words are often unintelligible. The primary audience of television professionals is those of the younger generation. Hence, the slang terms and idioms used are geared to reach this audience. How often I've heard, "That's so cool" or "Awesome!" Often they will end sentences with a preposition. Please, use grown-up language. But again, I digress.

A habit is a routine way of thinking, feeling, or behaving, which tends to occur unconsciously. I'm not a golfer, but I know that no player intentionally raises up on the backswing. To do so will ensure that the golfer will top the ball and make a weak shot in doing so. Yet this is among the most common errors on the course. Other common mistakes can be applied to any game or sport. In bowling, I will inadvertently turn my right hand over as I deliver the ball down the lane. This causes the ball to drift to the left and away from the pocket. A hitter in baseball could describe many bad habits that would prevent a batter from connecting solidly with the pitch. You get the point I'm making.

Similarly, as a speaker, you would never consciously clench your hands, pace the floor, jingle change or keys in your pockets, and avoid eye contact with the audience, as your listeners would inevitably be distracted and perceive you as nervous and insecure. With all this in mind, here are some public speaking habits I think presenters should keep in mind:

Speak distinctly and clearly. When a speaker is nervous and uncomfortable the tendency is to speak fast to get through the speech as soon as possible. This often results in slurred words making what is said garbled and incoherent. Slow down and take your time. Use silence as a useful rhetorical device. Many speakers have the bad habit of rushing through their content. The causes are often anxiety, adrenalin, or time constraints. Regardless of the reason, the three times you definitely want to pause include: before and after you say something significant which you want your audience to remember; before and after you transition from one key talking point to the next; and between your opening, main body, and closing. You want your audience to hear and understand the entire message you're trying to convey.

Design your talk to your audience. Benjamin Disraeli once said, "Talk to a man about himself, and he will listen for hours." In other words, if you don't talk to your audience about themselves, about their problems and needs, they most likely won't listen. Ask yourself: "Who is my audience? What are their burning issues? How does my message help them? How much do they know about my topic? What will I ask them to do in response to my message?" Listeners know when the speaker has not done their homework, and their responses range from disappointment and frustration to anger and boredom. All the best practices in public speaking depend upon this tenet: *Know Your Audience.*

Look at your audience when speaking. Many speakers fail to maintain meaningful, sustained eye contact with their listeners. Even though, unconsciously, their eyes scurry from person to person, darting around the room, they never pause actually to see the recipients of their message. A lack of eye contact implies a list of offenses: insincerity, disinterest, detachment, insecurity, shiftiness, and even arrogance. Looking at members of your audience, making good eye contact, says, "I have some helpful information for you. I share it because I care about you." Effective eye communication is the most crucial nonverbal skill in a speaker's toolbox.

Rehearse what you're going to say. In my ecclesiastical world, that's the same as practicing what you're going to preach. The most proficient speakers prepare. That is, they know the topic, have organized their content, and study their notes. The bad habit of not preparing results in the audience seeing and hearing an unrefined run-through as opposed to a finessed final performance. Though I use a manuscript for my sermons, I will practice the entire presentation aloud several times the week before Sunday so that I only have to glance at my notes occasionally during the speech. Moreover, this familiarity with my topic allows for a more casual, spontaneous approach in my delivery.

Deliver your speech with enthusiasm and energy. As the Guinness World Record holder for the most performances in the same Broadway show, George Lee Andrews is famous for playing the role of Monsieur André in "The Phantom of the Opera." Can you imagine saying the same lines, singing the same songs in his 9,382 performances? Yet he maintained the same level of energy and enthusiasm considering his contract was renewed 45 times over 23 years. Enthusiasm, defined as eager enjoyment and active interest, is an audience's most desired trait in a presenter. Conversely, a dull delivery—evidenced by a low monotone voice, bland facial expressions, and overall lethargy—is their most disliked trait. Crank up the energy level. Speak expressively. Smile sincerely. Enjoy the moment.

Open with a bang. Invest the thought, time and effort to craft and memorize a powerful opening. It's a common bad habit for speakers to waste those precious opening seconds rambling pointlessly, telling a joke, reading an agenda, apologizing needlessly, all of which fail to grab the audience's attention and motivate them to listen. You, your message, and your audience deserve much more. Tell an engaging relevant story, state a startling statistic, or ask a thought-provoking question. Oh, and if you do tell a joke, make sure it fits with your message and that it's going to be humorous for everyone in your audience.

Learn how to use the microphone. Speakers, unfamiliar with the use of hand-held sound amplifying devices, either hold it too close or away from the mouth to be effective. In one church I served, the sound equipment personnel suggested treating the hand-held device as "if you were going to lick an ice cream cone." Good advice. If using a stationary device or neck microphone, be sure to do a sound level check with the operator before your speech. Nothing is more distracting to an audience than trying to listen to someone unfamiliar with the use of sound equipment.

Finally, use proper grammar. I find a program called Grammarly extremely helpful. This program makes suggestions for contextual spelling, punctuation, sentence structure, style, and vocabulary enhancement. I don't use all of its recommendations, but most of them polish my writings to a greater degree. I've mentioned this before, but if you are going to quote someone in your speech, make sure you pronounce their name correctly. Use the dictionary or help from Google to get the right pronunciation and then spell it out phonetically in your notes or manuscript. When quoting a reference or person it's not necessary to say, "And I quote…" or "Quote… End quote." Rather than give the name of a book as a reference for a story used, I will usually just say, "The story is told about…" Most of the time your speech will be an informal presentation and not a scholarly dissertation requiring footnotes and documentation.

I'll close this story with a hymn that comes from our Methodist cousins across the pond in the United Kingdom. I first heard it when I exchanged churches with an English pastor in the summer of 2002. It's a beautiful, simple hymn written by Frances Ridley Havergal (1836-79), and is taken from a copy of *Hymns and Psalms* prepared by representatives of the British Methodist Conference and by members of the Baptist Union, Churches of Christ, Church of England, Congregational Federation, Methodist Church in Ireland, United Reformed Church, and the Wesleyan Reform Union. Whew!

Master, Speak! Thy Servant Heareth

Master, speak! Thy servant heareth,
Waiting for thy gracious word,
Longing for thy voice that cheereth;
Master, let it now be heard.
I am listening, Lord, for thee;
What hast thou to say to me?
WORDS: Frances Ridley Havergal, 1867 (1 Sam. 1-10)

48

Roasts

HAVING SERVED NINE CHURCHES in my fifty years (so far) of ordained ministry, we have experienced nine occasions when we have been welcomed to a new congregation and eight times when we have said "goodbye" as we departed a beloved people on our way to a new adventure. These experiences have been wearing and stressful for our entire family. Most times, when leaving a church, I have requested that those speaking at our departure banquet be lighthearted with their words, humorous and not mushy and oversentimental. This request was not only for our family's benefit but for everyone else's, too.

Some of these "roasts" have been memorable. The one with the church in Yuma, Arizona, was a riot! I never laughed so hard in my life. The whole atmosphere that evening was joyful and memorable. It was a delightful celebration of our four years together and a humorous tribute that Martha and I will never forget.

I have told Martha that the last twelve years of my ministry were some of the very best. They were healing and affirming. I grew in God's love through people that genuinely cared about their pastor. We cared and loved each other. My pastoral skills and knowledge were honed, and I pushed those two congregations—Cross Roads and Willowbrook—to risk taking new approaches to ministry and mission opportunities. We accomplished much for God's purposes of love and reconciliation, and I felt a stronger sense of maturing as a disciple of Jesus Christ, a confirming feeling of sanctification taking place within.

When I retired in 2004, a celebration of ministry was held at one of the country clubs in Sun City. Though I requested the same "roast" format, what was different this time was the fact that some members of my family—my father, sister, and brother—were going to be on the agenda. Uh oh, I smelled trouble!

The following is what my family contributed with my younger brother serving as the primary instigator:

Brother: *"I would like to start this presentation by asking everyone just two questions. By a show of hands, how many were surprised by Jim's retirement announcement? Thank you. Now, how many of you were surprised by Jim's announcement that he was quitting his job, going back to school, attending seminary, and wanted to become a minister? Our entire family! (About a third of the gathering raised their hands too!)*

"As you can see, this is not going to be an unbiased presentation—it is not going to be 'fair and balanced.' We can't all be the Fox News network. Although we were much surprised by Jim and Martha's decision to enter the ministry, we did think that he displayed many attributes that a minister should have. Among those attributes that Jim displayed at an early age are: 1) his power of persuasion, 2) showing compassion for those incarcerated, 3) he was a natural teacher, 4) he showed a keen ability in fundraising, and finally, 5) he was willing to take on any challenge.

"With the help of my father and sister, we will elaborate on each of these early childhood attributes of Jim's that he has honed enabling him to become your spiritual mentor. We do not want your praise nor your pity for the hardships we have endured during Jim's travels toward the ministry. Can't you just feel the love in this room?

"First, I will talk about Jim's power of persuasion.

"Martha Backus was one of the most beautiful, the smartest and talented young girls to come out of Sweetwater High School in National City, California. She could and still does sing like an angel. I kid you not! She was, for the average male, considered unapproachable. Jim, on the other hand, was never lacking in nerve. He actually asked Martha out on a date, and later asked her to marry him. The only reason I can think of as to why Martha said, 'Yes,' to his proposal is his power of persuasion, or could he have just worn her down by continually asking her to marry him?

"How many in this room have gone up against Jim's power of persuasion or have been worn down by Jim continually asking you to be on the Staff-Parish Relations or other committees? I know that Lucille and Bev have. Now that he's retiring, I don't want your phone calls complaining about my brother. As a matter of fact, please take my number off your speed "dials.

"Next, my dad will relate Jim's compassion for those incarcerated."

Father: *"Much like Paul, Silas, and Martin Luther King, Jr., my son Jim has spent time in jail. His jail time occurred early in life. We were living in a suburb of San Diego, a beach community, at the time. Jim was ten or eleven years old. He and a neighbor friend were always together.*

"I received a phone call from the local police department. They had received a complaint from an elderly man stating that two boys were stealing apricots from his orchard. The police arrived, and both were apprehended.

"The police sergeant said they wanted to put a scare into the boys. So they were placed in the police cruiser and put into an empty cell at one of their substations. They wanted me to pick up the boys immediately! They were having too much fun flushing the toilet in the cell and laughing as it echoed throughout the jailhouse. They were driving the police crazy.

"I don't know if it taught Jim a lesson in compassion, or if the lesson learned was how to make the best of a bad situation. His actions wouldn't have shown much sympathy had there been other prisoners."

Brother: *"Now, I want to say something about Jim as a natural teacher.*

"As memory serves me, we had recently moved from the Federal Housing Project in Pacific Beach to our first home in National City. Jim came home from junior high school and was flushed with excitement over all the new judo holds and escapes he had learned in P.E. class. I was greeted with, 'Put your hands on my neck and choke me.' I told him I really didn't want to. He insisted (that persuasion thing again). I relented, or was worn down and proceeded to choke my big brother. Jim turned white, then red and finally purple. The next thing I remember was being on the ground, my mouth was bleeding, and I was seeing stars for the first time in my life. Jim hit me, using a judo technique that I have never seen to this day.

"As you can guess, the lesson I learned that day had nothing to do with judo. Jim was an excellent teacher. He came by it naturally. It was only natural that he should punch me in the mouth in order for him to breathe.

"Now I'm going to ask my sister to the mike to relate Jim's early entries into the world of fundraising, one that's so important to the church today."

Sister: *"My brother Jim has always been fascinated with fundraising ideas and schemes. He seemed to have one every summer, and it always involved my younger brother and me. One of his better ideas, according to Jim, was his backyard carnivals. He would invite the neighborhood kids over and charge them the going rate to watch performances. My younger brother and I were the performances. Two acts that I still have nightmares about were the boxing exhibitions and the knife (ice pick) throwing demonstrations.*

"The boxing started when Jim received a pair of Joe Palooka boxing gloves for Christmas. They were the size of pillows. He made a boxing ring in the garage, obtained a stopwatch, and our training began. We were to box for three-minute rounds, one-minute rest between rounds, for ten rounds. The neighborhood kids loved it. There was one brutal summer in 1952 when we punched each other silly. Our brother, Don King, made a mint but my younger brother is still having short-term memory problems.

"Another act that was more dangerous and lucrative was the 'ice pick throwing.' Jim would line us up against the garage door, stand back a few yards (actually, no more than six inches), and throw the ice pick close to our bodies. We drew the line when he suggested to the crowd that he blindfold himself.

"In all the backyard carnivals, I don't remember receiving any of the proceeds. Jim said they went to a higher order, but he always seemed to have enough money for an ice cream bar after school."

Brother: *"Jim was always up for a challenge. My sister and I were born in San Diego. Jim, on the other hand, was from the old country, Scottsbluff, Nebraska. It was while on a family vacation to Scottsbluff that we really took notice of Jim's attribute of taking on any challenge.*

"We had arrived in Scottsbluff and were staying with our Great Aunt and Uncle on their farm. Our Great Uncle was showing us kids around the farm. In passing, he mentioned that we should stay away from the horse in the corral, for it was only 'half broke.' Jim's eyes glazed over and whispered to me, 'Let's break the other half.' I thought, 'He's so brave.' He opened the corral gate and walked straight in, with me following. The horse turned, put his ears back, and charged us. I was about trampled twice. First by Jim and then the horse. The horse was loose and wild. My winded dad and Great Uncle finally caught up to the exhausted horse after a chase through plowed fields. Somehow, in

family lore, this story is always called, 'The Time I Let the Horse Out.' Thank you for letting me set the account straight tonight!

"In conclusion, Jim really was an exceptional son to our parents and brother to my sister and me. We are all proud of both Jim and Martha. We have enjoyed watching and interacting with their children and seeing them develop into great parents themselves.

"In retirement, Jim and Martha will have a new and just as demanding lifestyle that will include a big dose of family. My wish for Jim and Martha in retirement is what I'll call the 'John Wesley Retirement.' He said, 'Do all the good you can, by all the means you can, in all the ways you can, in all the places you can, at all the times you can, to all the people you can, as long as ever you can.' Happy retirement!"

I hoped you enjoyed that presentation. I certainly did even though a bit of hyperbole was included. My father is no longer living, but I was blessed with great parents (my mother died a few years before I retired). My sister, brother, and I have a beautiful relationship, and when we get together, there's a lot of laughter and love. What a family!

I'll close with the fourth verse of this beautiful hymn:

Jesus, United by Thy Grace
Touched by the lodestone of thy love,
let all our hearts agree,
and ever toward each other move,
and ever move toward thee.

WORDS: Charles Wesley, 1742

49

United or Untied?

RELAX, I'M NOT GOING TO BE WRITING any political rant regarding the current situation in our nation, even though the title of this chapter might suggest as much. Our country is divided, the two main parties have forgotten about bipartisanship in efforts to solve problems in America, campaigns have become nastier and mean-spirited, and the people of this land have become more frustrated with and have shown an angrier resentment toward our government in Washington, D.C. To write about this topic is tempting but it's not my purpose. Even so, this chapter will probably be the most controversial of this book.

When I moved my family to Denver, Colorado, in June of 1968 to begin my seminary studies, a merger of the Evangelical United Brethren Church and The Methodist Church had taken place a few months earlier. We now had a new name—The United Methodist Church. Many former EUBs were disenchanted with this merger, and I remember seeing a cartoon in one of our denomination's publication, *The Interpreter* magazine (now discontinued), that showed an outdoor church sign that read, "First Untied Methodist Church." A puzzled pastor and church member are viewing the sign, and underneath was this caption, "That could possibly be correct."

Now, fifty years later, The United Methodist Church is at a crossroads. We are a divided church much like our nation, and the truth is, we are a hurting church as is our country. The issue: Homosexuality. More to the point, it's how our denomination will treat LGBTQ (lesbian, gay, bisexual, transgender, and questioning or queer) members and clergy. This concern has become a front and center controversy that threatens to split our church in two. Our General Conference will deal with this issue in 2019, but the possibility that we could become a church "untied" is a great possibility.

Throughout the history of our country our denomination has gotten sidetracked, confused, hostile, divided, and sometimes split over other issues. These include: 1) bitterly taking sides during the American Revolution (many pastors and church members were Tories, faithful to King George; 2) slavery (some of our Methodist bishops owned slaves; 3) the Civil War (some approved dividing the nation); 4) Women's Suffrage (some wanted to deny women the right to vote); 5) wine usage at Holy Communion (Welch's Grape Juice was the alternative); 6) preachers smoking (not in our church you won't); 7) divorced preachers (here's a no-no); 8) Temperance Sunday (no drinking, selling, or making alcohol and serving); 9) integration of Public Schools (it just won't work); 10) fear of AIDS (dirty needles are often the culprit, not sex partners); and 11) Same-Sex Marriage (should be outlawed). Moreover, in the church of my youth, the pastor and church membership frowned on dancing, though other Methodist pastors and churches in our denomination thought differently.

The incredible thing about these controversial issues is that they have been supported or opposed by use of biblical proof-texting. Passages from the Hebrew Bible (Old Testament) were given more weight than those in the New Testament, even Jesus' words. Or Paul's opinions given more credit than Jesus' teachings. It just depended on your point of view.

I'm not going to reference the biblical passages used in pro and con arguments and debates, you can Google these for yourself. Suffice it to say, neither side is ever swayed by their opponents' biblical and theological rationale, leaving no room for compromise.

In a recent Public Broadcasting Service two-part television special on the life of Mark Twain (Samuel Clemens) and filmed by Ken Burns, it was stated that Twain created quite a stir (euphemism for "hullabaloo") when in 1885 he published, *The Adventures of Huckleberry Finn*. The book was widely criticized upon release because of its extensive use of coarse language. Throughout the 20th century, and despite arguments that the protagonist and the tenor of the book are anti-racist, criticism of the book continued due to both its perceived use of racial stereotypes and its frequent use of a racial slur. The book was banned in some communities, and local libraries refused to have it on their shelves.

However, the controversy that upset many was that Mark Twain cunningly exposed the evils of slavery and racism, portraying the runaway slave, Jim, not as a thing to be owned, overlooked, humiliated, and denigrated, but as a human being. The PBS program, through the various experts on Twain's life, shared the fact that he had not attended Sunday school as a child or youth, that he wasn't influenced in any proper "Christian" upbringing. Therefore, Sam Clemens thought, his character wasn't contaminated by hypocritical persons within the church of his day. I thought it to be quite an indictment of, "Those who say, 'I love God,' and hate their brothers and sisters ... for those who do not love a brother or sister whom they have seen, cannot love God whom they have not seen." (1 John 4:20.)

Nevertheless, I'm a product of the church. My parents, who personified Christian ideals, saw to it that I grew up attending Sunday school. Vacation Bible School, youth group, camping for youth, Sunday morning and evening worship, and Youth for Christ rallies were also a part of my life. All these activities had a positive influence on my life and paved the way for the call to ministry that came to me unexpectedly but not surprisingly. Well, actually it did surprise me. The point is, I've learned to expect wonderful surprises from God's revealing love in the Holy Spirit. And as I've grown in Christian maturity and have become stronger in the process of sanctification, I have slowly (sometimes reluctantly) "... put an end to childish ways." (1 Corinthians 13:11.)

One of those ways has been my view of homosexuals, or to use the contemporary term LGBTQ. As previously mentioned, my best friend in childhood was a boy who turned out to be gay. Later as an adult, he joined the U.S. Navy but was given a general discharge (not honorary) because of his sexual orientation. The last I heard of him was through my mother who had received a letter from his mother. He had taken his own life. I think he couldn't stand the condemnation and ridicule because of the way he was wired from birth.

We have a young man in our family who is gay. He is a delightful person, sensitive and caring, one who shares my sense of humor (remember, don't be prejudiced). But there are others in our family, devout in the Christian faith, who treat him as a "sinner" and will have nothing to do with him. What's wrong with this picture?

Though Paul condemns a variety of sexually immoral offenders in his letter to the Corinthians, he also speaks of being justified by faith in his letter to the Galatians:

> *But now that faith [in Christ] has come, we are no longer subject to a disciplinarian, for in Christ Jesus you are all children of God through faith. As many of you as were baptized into Christ have clothed yourselves with Christ. There is no longer Jew or Greek, there is no longer male and female; for all of you are one in Christ Jesus. (Galatians 3:25-28.)*

The United Methodist Church is working diligently to resolve these issues with the LGBTQ community and same-sex marriages ("holy unions") that are being performed by some of its pastors. Our differences regarding this important and sensitive topic have become painfully apparent. A special General Conference will be held in February 2019, to settle the dispute. Presently, our bishops have been holding meetings with church leaders and laity to talk about "A Way Forward." Other policy models range from modifying some of the restrictive wording in the *Book of Discipline,* "One Church;" to eliminating it altogether, "The Simple Plan." Denominational leaders hope that one of these models now on the table, or some proposal not yet conceived, will avoid congregations leaving the denomination entirely. Instead, they hope the church will embrace the Methodist tradition that people can love Jesus, love their neighbors, and yet sometimes disagree.

Okay, I admit that I did some of my own proof-texting. Depending on your point of view, you haven't been swayed much, have you? At least you know where I stand. Although I, too, am hopeful that a reasonable compromise will be achieved, I'm not optimistic that The United Methodist Church I love and into which I was nurtured and eventually ordained will remain whole. I pray that it will survive and thrive, though I still don't understand the continued judgmental and condemning attitudes of some to be demonstrative of Jesus' example and teachings. Harsh words and name-calling have already been spoken. Liberals against conservatives, left-wingers against right-wingers, reformers versus reactionaries, charges of Revisionist Gay Theology, and on it goes. Sound familiar?

In the New Testament, the Pharisees plotted to entrap Jesus again and again. One of them, a lawyer, asked Jesus a question to test him:

> *"Teacher, which commandment in the law is the greatest?"*
> *He said to him, "'You shall love the Lord your God with all*
> *your heart, and with all your soul, and with all your mind.'*
> *This is the greatest and first commandment. And a second*
> *is like it: 'You shall love your neighbor as yourself.' On these*
> *two commandments hang all the law and the prophets."*
> *(Matthew 22:36-40.)*

A popular hymn in our church says it best: "I will break their hearts of stone, give them hearts for love alone. I will speak my word to them." To this, I say, "Come, Lord Jesus. Come."

We cannot continue to treat those within the LGBTQ community as things to be ignored, humiliated, ridiculed, and denigrated. Is the letter of the law more important than the spirit of the law? Instead, are we not all children of God through faith? Will mercy prevail over judgment? Do not all God's children deserve to be treated with dignity, respect, and love? This bewilderment on my part has slowly led me down a different path, and I have shifted and finally taken myself out of the camp of judgment. The result is that I feel a new freedom granted by Jesus the Christ.

Jesus, United by Thy Grace

Jesus, united by thy grace and each to each endeared,
with confidence we seek thy face and know our prayer is heard.
This is the bond of perfectness, thy spotless charity;
O let us, still we pray, possess the mind that was in thee.

WORDS: Charles Wesley, 1742

⸙ 50 ⸙

Mistakes (a sermon)

LATELY, I HAVE BEEN THINKING ABOUT the number "50." Not because this is the fiftieth and last story in this composition. No, specifically I was pondering 50 years ago... 1968. This was the year some have described as "The Year that Shattered America." There were marches for civil rights, the U.S.S. Pueblo incident, opposition to our country's involvement in the Vietnam War, the assassinations of Martin Luther King, Jr. and Robert Kennedy, and the Soviet Union's invasion of Czechoslovakia. It was a tumultuous time.

1968 was also when the Evangelical United Brethren Church merged with The Methodist Church to become The United Methodist Church. That same year, at the age of twenty-nine, I graduated from California Western University and moved Martha and our two children to Denver, Colorado, to begin post-graduate work at The Iliff School of Theology. Moreover, while attending seminary, I would serve as a student pastor to a small congregation. Fifty years ago... It doesn't seem possible.

Lots of pleasant remembrances and positive experiences over the past fifty years. Some beautiful people in the nine congregations to which I was appointed, including the one in Sun Lakes in retirement. All in all, when I look back, there is a profound sense of gratitude to God. It's nice to reminisce, but it can be a dangerous little game because something else intrudes. There are a few adverse recollections as well, very few. But isn't it strange how the negative things we encounter in life can obscure the good ones and dominate our thoughts? Why did I say what I said to that person? Why did I take the action I took? Why did I make that decision?

Things I did and said that hurt and brought an angry response. Things that disappointed and brought regret. Have you come across the same in your life?

With this in mind, I share a sermon that I gave as I completed fifty years of "holding God's people in my heart":

Shaking Off the Dust of Failure
2 Corinthians 12:6-10
Mark 6:7-13

"I think nothing's more difficult to face and admit to than failure. Part of this is because our society is so success-oriented that to fail makes one feel like a failure and to lose makes one feel like a loser. So we've become masters of the cover-up and experts at rationalization. When our Marines were pulled out of Lebanon several years ago, the Defense Department said that 'we backloaded our augmentation personnel.' The Rolls-Royce Company in Great Britain, unwilling to admit that their luxury automobiles ever break down, say instead that occasionally one of their cars 'will not proceed.' And then there's the father who said to his teenage son, 'I'm concerned about you being at the bottom of your class.' The son replied, 'Don't worry, Dad. They teach the same thing at both ends.'

"Of course, we in the church are not excluded from this form of self-deception. We find any excuse possible to explain away our failures and flops, blaming the age in which we live, the evil influence of television or the Internet, or people's differing lifestyles and their lack of commitment. But wouldn't it be better to admit our shortcomings and face up to our failures? I like the article that appeared in a church newsletter and read, 'If God gave you a good singing voice, come and join our choir. If God gave you a lousy singing voice, join our choir anyway and get even.' There's nothing wrong with shortcomings, with falling flat on our faces in failure, with making mistakes. Where did we ever get the idea that to be successful means never failing and never making mistakes?

"Some of you remember John Wooden, the coach for UCLA, whose teams dominated college basketball for many years. He was interviewed and asked about his coaching philosophy that produced so many successful teams and individual champions. Wooden quoted his own coach at Purdue, Ward Lambert, who said, 'The team that makes more mistakes will be the winner because the team that makes more mistakes will be playing harder.'

"Our Scripture lesson this morning speaks to this truth about life and faith. It locates Jesus in Galilee as he sends out the disciples two by two on their appointed mission. His marching orders are a challenge that requires risk and danger. He promises the disciples a struggle in which they could expect rejection, failure and empty results. So he says to them, 'If any place will not welcome you and they refuse to hear you, as you leave, shake off the dust that is on your feet as a testimony against them.' The disciples could expect failure, but it wasn't to discourage them. They were to shake off the dust from their feet and move on. We need to remember that God offers us the grace of beginning again so that we can confront our failures and disappointments and make the most of them. Therefore, I want to share a few thoughts this morning that may help us in our living when we find ourselves shaking off the dust of failure.

"First, we need to be aware that failure is an unavoidable part of human experience. That's our first word. I once heard a high school commencement speaker say, 'Failure is a word found only in the vocabulary of fools and cowards.' I winced when I heard that because failure is not only found in the vocabulary of *everyone who is alive,* but it's a part of our authentic experience. To live is to face the contradictions and mysteries of our world. To live is to meet and deal with the conflicts and problems of sharing life with each other, of being together, of trying to understand each other. And in such encounters and sharing, failures and disappointments are inescapable. No one of us is perfect. We're creatures of mixed motives. We have our shadow sides that distort our expectations and understandings. We have our limitations and our prejudices, our defenses and our selfish needs that influence our responses and help decide our decisions.

"Moreover, life is full of events beyond our control, and we never know how or when they'll break in upon us to change or destroy our best-laid plans. Wars, natural disasters, birth and death, illness and other personal tragedies, economic and social upheavals, and some other crises reveal how uncertain and unpredictable life is. How suddenly it all can end in failure and disappointment for us. There are many things beyond our control.

"Garrison Keillor of 'Prairie Home Companion' radio fame shares a poem about how his ancestors set out for Oregon and only got as far as Minnesota and how his great-grandfather had died with that dream still unfulfilled in him. For everyone, there are uncrossed mountains, goals that were lost, disappointments that came to us and defeats that left their marks on our lives. To be alive is to fail, to make mistakes, to live with regret and wonder what might have been.

"Second, we're reminded that life goes on and, by God's grace, we can go on with it. Keillor's great-grandfather labored hard in Minnesota, despite his lost dream. Life went on for him, and he went on with it. No failure is so final that it makes us a failure. We can learn from our failures as we pick up the pieces and begin again. We can find meanings in our defeats and disappointments that teach us and prepare us for the next opportunity. That's why a corporate executive told his employees:

> *Double your rate of failure. Failure is not the enemy of success. Failure is the teacher. You can be undone by failure, or you can learn from it. So go ahead and make some daring mistakes by risking the new. Make as many as you want, because that's where we find fulfillment—on the far side of failure.*

"Strengths of character, moral power, and maturity in us depend more on our failures than on our achievements, more on what we've lost than on what we've accomplished. Someone once said, 'The greatest strengths and weaknesses of gifted leaders hinge most on how they responded and lived through failure and defeat.' That was true of Moses, wasn't it? And David? And Isaiah, along with the other prophets? It was true of the apostle Paul, wasn't it? Paul wrote:

> *Three times I appealed to the Lord about this (thorn in the flesh), that it would leave me, but he said to me, "My grace is sufficient for you, for power is made perfect in weakness." So, I will boast all the more gladly of my weaknesses, so that the power of Christ may dwell in me. Therefore I am content with weaknesses, insults, hardships, persecutions, and*

calamities for the sake of Christ; for whenever I am weak,
then I am strong. (2 Corinthians 12:8-10).

It was also true of Martin Luther, wasn't it? And Beethoven? And Madame Curie at her 497th unsuccessful experiment with radium? And Elizabeth Fry in her lifelong crusade to reform prisons? It was also true of Alan Paton in his bitter struggle for racial justice in South Africa.

"The moral stature, the depth of character, and the integrity of example in such persons emerges out of how they handled failure and loss, frustration and disappointment. They didn't fall back into the shadow of their goal posts when defeat came upon them. Instead, they found their way back to the line of scrimmage and continued their struggle.

"Some of you may remember the news story of five fishermen from Costa Rica who were adrift for five months in a tiny boat in the Pacific Ocean, men who reached the limits of human endurance and despair. At one point one of them wrote this farewell message to his wife:

The rainwater that we had is about used up. We have no
food. We have suffered so much that I believe, with death,
God will finally allow us to rest … I only know one thing—I
will love you … I no longer have the strength to go on.

But they did go on, for *three more months*—and one reason they survived is that they trusted God and upheld each other. Remember that when we find ourselves trying to shake off the dust of failure, life still goes on and, by God's grace we can go on with it.

"Finally, we need to commit our failures and struggles to God's power and endurance and claim God's power for beginning again. When we entrust ourselves and our shortcomings to God, the power does come. The persistence of the human soul through God's strength of grace is incredible, as the story of the fishermen declares. We may think our failure has made us a failure and there's no more tomorrow for us. Then God opens a door, sends us someone to love or rescue us, speaks to us the word we need, gives us a fresh possibility and renews in us the power to stay with it and not give up.

"We see this in Jesus and his ministry. Almost from the very beginning, Jesus faced opposition and frustration at every turn. His own townspeople tried to drive him out of Nazareth. His own family tried to persuade him to give up his mission. The religious establishment put every obstacle they could think of in his way and sought any means to oppose him and his work. They finally plotted to kill him. His disciples and followers didn't understand him and tried to hinder him. One of them betrayed him and another denied him, and at the final countdown, they all ran away to save their own skins. To God, Jesus entrusted life's reversals and disappointments, its indifference and distortions, and he moved against them and through them, revealing how love may fail in doing what it sets out to do, but, by God's grace, love always succeeds in being what it sets out to be. So it is with us. God is the God of failures, but with the power to redeem them and with a grace that enables us to begin again.

"The story of Dr. Tom Dooley is one that many in my generation will never forget. His heroic mission of medicine in Laos was marked by failure, setbacks, disappointments, and mistakes. And then he was diagnosed as having cancer and fought its assault on the body, gradually growing weaker, but refusing to fall back to the shadow of his goal posts. He kept saying, 'I'm not quitting. If I stop now, I will die sooner.' Dooley finally collapsed while working twenty hours a day in the hospital in Laos, was brought back to New York, the day after his thirty-fourth birthday, and died. Around his neck was a St. Christopher's medal with the familiar words of Robert Frost engraved on the back of it:

> *The woods are lovely, dark and deep*
> *But I have promises to keep,*
> *And miles to go before I sleep,*
> *And miles to go before I sleep.*

Shake off the dust from your feet and move on. No failure is final. God in Jesus Christ goes with us. We are never alone. Amen!"

I'll close with a hymn usually sung when a pastor leaves a congregation to go to another church or retires. I include all four verses. It's especially sad when the people and pastor love each other dearly. In the meantime, recalling my estimated ancestry background: *Slán* (Irish)... *Farvel*

(Danish)... *Auf Wiedersehen* (German)...*Cheerio* (English)... *Vaya con Dios* (Spain)... *Ciao* (Italian)... αντιο σας (Greek)... and *Shalom* (Jewish).

God Be with You till We Meet Again

God be with you till we meet again;
by his counsels guide, uphold you,
with his sheep securely fold you;
God be with you till we meet again.
God be with you till we meet again;
neath his wings securely hide you,
daily manna still provide you;
God be with you till we meet again.
God be with you till we meet again;
when life's perils thick confound you,
put his arms unfailing round you;
God be with you till we meet again.
God be with you till we meet again;
keep love's banner floating o'er you,
smite death's threating wave before you;
God be with you till we meet again.

WORDS: Jeremiah E. Rankin, 1880

Notes

1   Brian Wheeler, *What happens at an atheist church?* (BBC News Magazine, 4 February 2013) https://www.bbc.com/news/magazine-21319945.

2   https://www.va.gov/opa/vetsday/vetdayhistory.asp.

3   Taken from "To Be United Methodist: What is 'itineracy'?" by the Ask the UMC team at http://www.interpretermagazine.org accessed on 20 September, Copyright © 2018, United Methodist Communications, Used by permission.

4   Michael Korda, *Clouds of Glory: The Life of Robert E. Lee,* (HarperCollins, 2014).

5   https://famouskin.com/famous-kin-menu.php?name=4640+robert+e+lee.

6   https://apps.ksbe.edu/kaiwakiloumoku/kaleinamanu/he-aloha-moku-o-keawe/kona_kai_opua.

7   Tony Campolo, *Is Jesus a Republican or a Democrat? And 14 Other Polarizing Issues,* (Word Publishing, 1995) 1-2.

8   Ibid, 2.

9   https://www.psychiatry.org/patients-families/alzheimers.

10 Anthony Doerr *All the Light We Cannot See,* (Scribner, 2014) 468.

11 *Author's note: I'm indebted for the first part of this chapter to material written by Norris Burkes, syndicated columnist, national speaker, and board-certified hospital chaplain with the Association of Professional Chaplains.*

12 Richard Dawkins, *The God Delusion,* (Houghton Mifflin Harcourt, 2006) 23-24.

13 Frederick Buechner, *The Hungering Dark,* (Harper and Row, 1985) 27-28.

14 Daniel Silva, *The English Spy,* (HarperCollins, 2015) 57-58.

15 https://en.wikipedia.org/wiki/Kahlil_Gibran.

16 William C. Martin, *The Art of Pastoring: Contemplative Reflections,* (CTS Press, 1994), 9.

17 Wayne Oates, *Pastoral Counseling,* (Westminster: John Knox Press, 1974) 100.

18 Henri J.M. Nouwen, *Reaching Out: The Three Movements of the Spiritual Life,* (Image Book: Doubleday, 1986) 45.

19 Tim Hansel, *You Gotta Keep Dancin',* (David C. Cook, 1985) 16-17.

20   Raquel Welch, *Raquel: Beyond the Cleavage,* (Weinstein Books, 2010) 265.

21   Max Lucado, *The Great House of God*, (Word Publishing, 1997) 159-161.

22   Adam Hamilton, *Creed: What Christians Believe and Why*, (Abingdon Press, 2016) 80.

23   Ibid, 81-82.

Printed in the United States
By Bookmasters